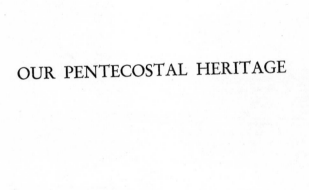

OUR PENTECOSTAL HERITAGE

Our

Pentecostal

Heritage

By

F. W. LEMONS

OUR PENTECOSTAL HERITAGE

Copyright, 1963, by Pathway Press

All rights reserved

FIRST EDITION

Library of Congress Catalog Card Number: 63-12492

Printed in the United States

DEDICATION

To Evelyn, my wife

INTRODUCTION

An increasing awareness of the Pentecostal experience has led ministers and members of Episcopalian, Methodist, Presbyterian, Baptist and other churches to receive the Holy Ghost baptism. Requests for information have impelled men to write on this Biblical doctrine. It is fitting, therefore, that F. W. Lemons a son of one of the pioneer preachers of Pentecost, M. S. Lemons, write this book. It has been my pleasure and honor to know the author as a dear friend for the past forty years. It has been an even greater honor to labor with him as a brother minister in the vineyard of the Lord.

His association with Pentecost is not only as a witness of God's moving, but also as a participant in this experience. As an active participant, F. W. Lemons became an able preacher and proponent of the Pentecostal experience. For the past thirty-seven years he has proclaimed this doctrine throughout these United States as pastor, state overseer, writer, Bible teacher and camp meeting speaker. He is, therefore, fully qualified to write such a book.

The purpose of the writer is to introduce others to this Pentecostal blessing. His logical approach will give one a thorough Biblical concept of this doctrine. A progressive unfolding of truth is set forth in a clear and convincing manner. His style of presentation is most refreshing and at the same time lucid and penetrating.

The last chapter of this book sums up all the facts presented and logically concludes that Pentecost is a perennial blessing available to all. It emphasizes that Pentecost will refresh our Christian experience and strengthen us in our journey toward heaven. It is my prayer that this book will bless its readers and that having read it, they will be persuaded to seek this glorious experience.

James A. Cross
Former General Overseer
Church of God

PREFACE

This work is humbly submitted in the hope that it may acquaint others with the Pentecostal blessing. No claim is made of a new revelation, because if it is new it is not true, and if it is true it is not new. All that is intended is the giving of a new look at some very precious old truth. "The foundation of every great revival is the discovery of some old truth."—Anon.

In view of the numerous books which have been written on the various phases of the Holy Spirit and Pentecost, it may appear presumptuous to add another. The apology for doing so is that the subject is almost inexhaustible and that it is being treated in this small volume in a manner few others have chosen to follow. The approach to the subject matter is different.

It is sent forth with earnest prayer that those who read may drink deeply at the Fountain of Living Water.

F. W. Lemons

CONTENTS

ERRATA

Unfortunately, three rather serious typographical errors appear in this otherwise excellent book. Page 30, paragraph 2, line 2, should read "center of stage" instead of "center of state." Page 46, paragraph 2, line 6, should read "the mystery of it" instead of "the misery of it." Page 78, paragraph 2, line 6, should read "have done disservice" instead of "have done this service."

CHAPTER I

PENTECOST PREFIGURED

PENTECOST was no mere accident of history. The occurrence on the Day of Pentecost was not merely incidental to history. It was as much a part of a well-defined plan as was Calvary and the crucifixion of Jesus Christ. It was as certainly a part of the eternal purpose of God as was the fact that Jesus Christ was the predestined Lamb of God slain from the foundation of the world.

One group of theological philosophers holds that the world is devoid of purpose, being a part of a "meaningless universe." Another group subscribing to the opposite position contends that there is purpose in God's universe, despite the apparent conflict and chaos; and that the purpose of God may be discovered, at least in part; and that, in the end, His purpose shall prevail. True wisdom is ever concerned with discovering and comprehending that purpose.

When Christianity first appeared, the world was under the influence of Greek philosophy which held the opinion of "the unmoved eternal order of ideas.

Immutable law, whether of nature or of society, represents to the senses the changeless eternity of the intelligible world. The phenomenon of movement itself is an imitation of immobility, being conceived as cyclical, both in the regular motions of the heavenly bodies and in the eternal recurrence which governs the course of history, so that the same events will be everlastingly repeated. By going round in a circle even change thus conforms to the stable eternity of the ideal world, and no longer implies innovation. No such thing as an event can ever infringe the eternal order."Jean Danielou, S. J. in *The Lord of History*.

The same author points out that there have been some positive contradictions of the melancholy Greek position of endless repetition. For instance in the Epistle to the Hebrews, Christ is said to have entered "once" into the holy place, that is, when He ascended into heaven. This was a radical deviation from the assumed "eternal order." "That event, then," says he, "has finally effected a qualitative change at a given moment in time, so that things can never be the same again." With that event there began to unfold the eternal purpose of God, "the mystery of His will" which in other ages had not been revealed.

The Word of God supports the position that there is purpose in history. That purpose may be hidden from our view, because history is written by fallible and biased scholars. Consequently much truth is lost to us in a milieu of errors and contradictions. But wise men with spiritual vision will observe that God still directs the affairs of men, and that He who causes even the wrath of men to praise Him is still at the controls. A careful observer will also see that there are invisible currents and forces which direct the course of history and which at strategic times have turned it back into its channel. The impact of Pentecost was such a force. On that day of New Testament fame a unique, supernatural force was released into the world to promulgate and to perpetuate the gospel until the purpose of God shall be consummated and Christ shall return to earth. Since that day the term *Pentecost* has not merely denoted a holiday of Hebrew folklore, but it has become the recognized and standing symbol of the advent of a power destined to guide the stream of history according to the eternal purpose of the Master Designer.

"So richly has God lavished upon us his grace He has granted us complete insight and understanding of the open secret of his will, showing us how it was the purpose of his design so to order it in the fulness of the ages that all things in heaven and earth alike should be gathered up in Christ—in the Christ in whom we have had our heritage allotted to us (as was decreed in the design of him who carries out everything according to the counsel of his will), to make us redound to the praise of his glory."—Ephesians 1:8-12, Moffatt Translation.

At the very heart and center of the plan of the

Supreme Architect was the advent of Jesus Christ to the World—Immanuel—God with us—the unfolding revelation of God in human flesh, finally giving Himself as a propitiation for the sins of the world. "History is His story" is a very wise maxim. Those who in their labyrinthian meanderings to accumulate knowledge have failed to consider Him as Lord of history are like the man who could not see the forest for the trees. But the story of Jesus Christ short of Pentecost is not the complete story. Pentecost is an indispensable integral in the divine plan of history.

A careless glimpse at a huge engineering project in which highway workmen are diligently blasting rock, burning brush and moving earth reveals little more than confusion and destruction and is a vexation to the motorist who has to detour over rough roads because of it. Who has not complained and inquired the reason for it? And the versatile "sidewalk engineers" have criticized simply because they did not understand the plan, which from their observation point, seemed purposeless. But somewhere there is a man with a blueprint. He pays little attention to the smoke, the dust, the blastings, or to the cheap advice from the sidelines. He understands the plan and realizes the fulfillment of a dream. Out of the maze he visions a continuous emergence of order according to previous design. If he be asked what he is doing, his answer will not be "blasting rock, burning brush, or moving dirt," but he will say that he is building a super highway. The man with the Word of God is the man with the blueprint. If he is a student of the Word he can see the wisdom of the plan of God and that out of the puzzling mysteries of time, the eternal purpose of God is taking form according to His design, all "to the praise of the glory of his grace."

Biased criticism of Pentecost has been abundant. It has filled the air with confusing explanations. The critics have darkened counsel with words. Granting that something momentous did occur in apostolic times as recorded in the Acts of the Apostles, to some critics it was only an incidental happening which was irrelevent to anything present or future, or a historical event which should be passed over with as little emphasis as possible. But Pentecost, like the rejected stone in the building of Solomon's Temple which was eventually discovered to be the chief cornerstone, fits perfectly into the divine pattern, and without it there is no explanation of the history of the church. It was an event of history with a lofty, far-reaching purpose. That purpose was the execution of the Great Commission. It was forever to be the norm of Christian faith. In spite of the fact of the finished work of redemption, the cross, the resurrection, the forty days the resurrected Lord was with His followers, and the grand ascension witnessed by them, Jesus commanded them to suspend all operations—even to postpone their world missions enterprise—until that day, long planned and set aside in the inter-theistic councils of the triune God for the descent of the Holy Ghost. The day, of course, was the Day of Pentecost.

Something very extraordinary was predestined for that day that would give impetus to the strange message the disciple-ambassadors were to carry to all nations and to the ends of the world. Not a single one of them dared venture forth without waiting for the fulfillment of the promise that they should "receive power" that would equip them for their stupendous mission of declaring the unsearchable riches of Christ—the Christ who was rejected, despised, crucified, but resurrected, forever living, seated at the right hand of the Majesty in glory, yet everywhere present. Such an astounding message, so fraught with mystery, intrigue and paradox would require supersensory authentication. The messengers would require extraordinary credentials. No man in his right mind would have dreamed of challenging the world that had so recently crucified the Leader of the insignificant little flock with a story so absurdly ridiculous and at once so marvelously sublime without the equipment Jesus told them they must have, and for which they must tarry in Jerusalem until that day.

Theirs was to be the task of making disciples of all men, of turning them from the power of Satan to God, and of getting their message "over" to such a degree that belligerent enemies of God would be constrained to repent and to become sons of God by faith in the crucified Saviour. Staggering task! But it was crystal clear to them that this feat could not be accomplished through ordinary processes of "worldly wisdom." And it is just as clear today that since men are still victims of sin, unbelief and ungodliness, and since the cure is just the same as it was when the first declaration of the evangel was proclaimed on the Day of Pentecost, that in order to have an approved, authenticated ministry that will cause men to cry, "What shall we do," those who will dare to speak for God should receive the same equipment prescribed for the first disciples.

The message of salvation is to a world that is as truly lost as it was when Jesus gave the Great Commission and is the same old story of His dying as the sinners' substitute; therefore we need not be surprised to know that the story of Pentecost with all its implications is still in vogue. Is it not presumptuous to attempt to carry on the work of God in the energy of the flesh or with the wisdom of the world alone, when in doing so we must ignore or proscribe the wisdom of God in providing the equipment? The message of redeeming love must be preached with "the Holy Ghost sent down from heaven."

It is little wonder, therefore, that so much is said of Pentecost in both the Old and the New Testaments, and that it is prefigured for us in Old Testament types, especially in the Jewish feasts. Its place and relationship among the Jewish feasts show something of the design of the Lord with reference to Pentecost and the plan of God for the entire scheme of redemption (see Leviticus 23). We shall not consider all the feasts. In short we shall examine the relation of the major feasts, their related sequences and what they prefigure.

The Passover

The Passover was a memorial, and brought into view redemption by blood, upon which all other blessings rest (Exodus 12:1-37). From the depths of remote antiquity has come this keystone of the Christian system. It stands for "Christ our passover . . . sacrificed for us," 1 Corinthians 5:7. It was a preview of Calvary and of the dying Lamb of God.

The Feast of Unleavened Bread

This one should be studied in connection with the Feast of the Passover, for it began the next day after the Passover and spanned a full week spent in feasting together. It speaks of communion with Christ, of the "holy walk" of consecration after conversion. Redemption is nothing if it does not lead to purification. Vainly do we eat the Paschal Lamb or sprinkle blood if it is not followed by purging out the old leaven. The feast lasted seven days—a full measure of time. We are to serve God in righteousness "all the days of our lives."

The Feast of Pentecost

The Feast of Pentecost is sometimes called the Feast of Weeks. It began seven full weeks plus one day after the Passover. Its other names are the Feast of Harvest, the Day of Firstfruits, or Feast of Firstfruits (Exodus 23:14-16). This feast was commemorated at the end of the wheat harvest. As such it marked the end of the old dispensation. It is significant that instead of the firstfruits offering, or sheaf offering, they offered a wave offering of two loaves. None of the grain of the recent harvest was to be eaten until the Pentecost loaves had been offered to the Lord (Leviticus 23:15-17; Numbers 28:26). These loaves show the result of the Passover—Christ crucified, resurrected. Without the Passover there could be no Pentecost. Without the time of sowing there could be no harvest. "Except a corn of wheat fall into the ground and die, it abideth alone: but if it die, it bringeth forth much fruit" (John 12:24).

1. Bread represents the Church, the result of the grain that died and sprung up again, bringing forth abundantly. "We being many are one bread, and one body: for we are all partakers of that one bread" (1 Corinthians 10:17). In the mystery of bread is a

very vivid object lesson revealing the mystery of the church. As the grains of wheat—the products of the grain that died and rose again in fruitful harvest— are brought together from every part of the field, milled, compounded and kneaded together to make bread, so the redeemed are brought together from every tribe and nation to Christ, made savory by the impartation of his divine nature, to form a new unity, "one bread," the Church.

2. The two loaves represent the firstfruits of a plenteous harvest of souls, the great awakening revival made possible by the death of the Passover Lamb, who afterward sent the Comforter.

It was not accidental that the time chosen for the Feast of Pentecost was just fifty days after the Passover. According to Jewish authorities the Law was given on the fiftieth day after Israel left Egypt. Pentecost, of course, means "fiftieth." Pentecost to them was the official ending of the old dispensation and the beginning of their history as a civilized nation with a code of laws and a system of civil government handed down to them from God on Mt. Sinai.

The Feast of Pentecost was a memorial of this very important event in the history of their transition from twelve nomadic tribes emerging from slavery, unable to govern themselves, to a chosen nation under God with a representative, judicial system of government of which Jehovah was their Lord and King.

In addition to being a perpetual memorial to Israel the Feast of Pentecost was a prophetic type of the great Pentecost to come in the "Fullness of Time" when the time should be ripe, fifteen hundred years later, and when the Lord would again send fire from heaven, not to engrave His laws upon tables of stone, but upon the hearts of his followers. This would be the operation of God's grace by which the Church should be born.

The Feast of Trumpets

This feast was celebrated by the sounding of the trumpet from morning until evening. Trumpets were used at all feasts and convocations of Israel, but only at the Feast of Trumpets were they heard in all their mightiness all the day long (Leviticus 23:24; Numbers 29:1). Significantly this feast immediately succeeded the Feast of Pentecost. It typifies the preaching of the Gospel, which is the next step after Pentecost. With the sounding of the trumpet began the new year; it announced almost every important occasion in connection with the Jewish worship, but not until after the glorious season of Pentecost did its combined tones break forth upon the ears of all men. Not until after the Pentecostal outpouring of the Holy Ghost was the good news of Christ crucified, dead, buried, resurrected and alive for evermore, exalted to the right hand of the Father, which was the burden of the great commission, shouted forth into all the world. Then it was uttered in a fullness which startled empires and thrilled the ages. It announced the Day of Atonement calling all men to reconciliation.

Pentecost is indeed one of the ancient landmarks, and is well within the boundaries of our inheritance.

CHAPTER II

THE PENTECOSTAL PROMISE

PRIOR to the Day of Pentecost the average citizen of Israel did not expect to share in deep spiritual experiences. According to the Old Testament the work of the Spirit is connected with the extraordinary and abnormal. It was not so much a daily power and presence as an abnormal phenomenon and manifestation, spasmodic and transitory. These manifestations "at sundry times and in divers manners" were not generally shared by the common people. So exceptional were they that the average Israelite had no cause to expect them. Being content to believe what they were taught, they were quite willing to deal with God through a mediator.

But sometimes—perhaps once in a generation— someone in a different role would appear. The Spirit of God would come upon him, and he would speak for God, and speak with authority. Such men knew God in a strange way. They shared the secret of the Lord. "Seers" and "prophets" they were called. These were the type men who wrote the Bible. "Holy men of God spake as they were moved by the Holy Ghost" (2 Peter 1:21). Someone has guessed, perhaps to one in a hundred thousand. In the time of Eli and Samuel it is recorded that "the word of the Lord was precious in those days; there was no open vision," explained in the marginal reference in some Bibles, "A word from the Lord was unusual in those days; there was no public vision" (1 Samuel 3:2). There was a period in the history of Israel of approximately four hundred years—from Malachi to John the Baptist—when no prophet appeared. It has been called "the long silence."

Early in the Bible, however, we are introduced to the Holy Spirit who is omnipresent, omnipotent, omniscient and eternal. He is the executive member of the divine trinity, who carries out the work of God on earth. In the Old Testament there are references to Him as an associate in Creation (Genesis 1:2, 26), as striving with man (Genesis 6:3), as enlightening (Job 32:8), and as imparting skill (Exodus 31:2-5; 28:3).

A glimpse of a scene in the camp of Israel will confirm the statement that while the Holy Spirit was everywhere present everyone was not a partaker of the Holy Spirit as is the privilege of every believer in the grace dispensation. Moses was the great, undisputed prophet and leader of Israel. The Spirit of God was indeed upon him. But one day an excited messenger, very zealous for the honor of Moses, hurried into his presence to announce the shocking news that two other men were in the camp prophesying. He expected Moses to respond with drastic action defending his sole right as possessor of the gift of the Spirit, to silence immediately the two presuming upstarts. But Moses who in spiritual stature stood head and shoulders above most of the great men of history and also bears the distinction of "the meekest man of all the earth" did nothing of the sort. His magnanimous heart rejoiced at the manifestation of the Spirit and he exclaimed, "Enviest thou for my sake? would God that all the Lord's people were prophets, and that the Lord would put his spirit upon them" (Numbers 11:29). Previously he had laid his hands upon seventy of the elders of Israel and the Spirit of God come upon them. Fifteen hundred years of the history of Israel are interspersed by the appearances of men upon whom abode the Spirit of God, and whose stories appear in the Old Testament.

Among those so favored of the Lord was the Prophet Joel who prophesied in Judah about 800 B.C. His prophecies range from lamentations and judgments to ecstatic promises of hope and assurance to all people. It was he who announced, "And it shall come to pass afterward, that I will pour out my spirit upon all flesh; and your sons and your daughters shall prophesy, and your old men shall dream dreams, and your young men shall see visions; And also upon the servants and upon the handmaidens in those days will I pour out of my Spirit" (Joel 2:28, 29).

It was a prophecy almost too good to be true that ordinary people—young men, old men and old women regardless of social station—should share in a glorious outpouring of God's Spirit just as the prophet had, and that they should prophesy, enjoy heavenly visions and dreams of the Spirit. It was fantastic. I' meant the elevation of the common people, the inexperienced youth, the aged, too old to claim position, the women who held little status in comparison with their husbands and brethren, the servants and handmaidens—at the bottom rung of the social ladder. It meant the destruction of all class barriers, so that the least in the kingdom of God would have equal rights with the highest and noblest of the aristocracy, kings or priests.

It took courage to make such a prediction in Joel's time, but it was good news to the masses. Joel was certain of its fulfillment and of a day when all kinds of people would receive the Holy Ghost. This very comprehensive and hopeful prophecy was in due time verified by others. For example:

"And I will pour upon the house of David, and upon the inhabitants of Jerusalem, the spirit of grace and of supplications" (Zechariah 12:10).

"For with stammering lips and another tongue will he speak to this people. To whom he said, This is the rest wherewith ye may cause the weary to rest;

and this is the refreshing: yet they would not hear"
(Isaiah 28:11).

It is quite patent according to St. Paul that this was
a reference to the Pentecostal experience (1 Corinthians 14:21).

About seven hundred years afterward came John
the Baptist, the voice in the wilderness proclaiming
the coming of the Messiah. The promise that had
inspired so much comfort and hope, and now so old
that many despaired of its fulfillment, was revived
by him. He confirmed it in no uncertain terms.

The stature of a witness may add to or detract
from the impact of testimony. John was an unim-
peachable witness of unsullied character. Jesus paid
high tribute to John, declaring he was no weakling
reed shaken by the popular breezes, and that "Among
them that are born of women there hath not risen
a greater than John the Baptist" (Matthew 11:11).
When Jesus presented himself to John to receive baptism at his hands it is quite evident that he did not
understand that Jesus was the long-awaited Messiah,
for the record states: "And John bare record, saying,
I saw the Spirit descending from heaven like a dove,
and it abode upon him. And I knew him not: but he
that sent me to baptize with water, the same said
unto me, Upon whom thou shalt see the Spirit descending, and remaining on him, the same is he which
baptizeth with the Holy Ghost" (John 1:32, 33).

It is not surprising, therefore, that John in true

humility before the august presence of his Lord reverently pleading his own unworthiness exclaimed, "I have need to be baptized of thee" (Matthew 3:14). The climax of the ministry of this the last and greatest of the Old Testament prophets was the announcement of the appearance of Jesus, and as a herald of God identifying Him officially to the people of His generation. John himself spirit-filled from birth, declared: "I indeed baptize you with water unto repentance: but he that cometh after me is mightier than I, whose shoes I am not worthy to bear: he shall baptize you with the Holy Ghost, and with fire" (Matthew 3:11). This utterance which was the very heart of the message of John was an added assurance that the day was near when the promise of the ancient prophets that the people should receive the Holy Ghost was about to be fulfilled.

Having fulfilled his mission John graciously retired from the center of the stage in deference to the Greater. The spotlight of Bible history then focused upon Jesus, who was the "Anointed" of God. He set out upon his ministry, "in the power of the Spirit." At a Sabbath service in his home town, Nazareth, he read from the prophecy of Isaiah (61:1) "The Spirit of the Lord is upon me, because he hath anointed me to preach the gospel." He indicated to the townfolk that this Scripture referred to him and that it was fulfilled in him. He is the great paragon of the Spirit-filled, Spirit-dominated life.

The hopes and fears of all the world were indeed destined to meet in Jesus Christ. This is especially true with reference to the coming of the Comforter. John had given him a particular distinction, "He that baptizeth with the Holy Ghost." This baptism was not delegated to human agency but was forever to remain the sole prerogative of Jesus Christ. He is still the mighty Baptizer. It should be observed that this blessing was to be received by faith in Him. He said the Father would send the Comforter "in my name." Those indisposed to recognize Him and to accord to him the highest place of honor, as the all-wise God worthy of our whole-hearted worship and devotion are in no position to receive the Comforter, whose function it is to "glorify" Jesus. Thus all the promises of God recorded in the Old Testament with reference to the future outpouring of the Holy Ghost are bound up in Him. This fact is further emphasized in his own statement on the last and great day of the Feast of Tabernacles which is recorded in John 7:37-39.

"In the last day, that great day of the feast, Jesus stood and cried, saying, If any man thirst, let him come unto me, and drink. He that believeth on me, as the scripture hath said, out of his belly shall flow rivers of living water. (But this spake he of the Spirit, which they that believe on him should receive: for the Holy Ghost was not yet given; because that Jesus was not yet glorified)."

The Feast of Tabernacles was one of the most joyous of Jewish festivals. It reached its climax on the last or the eighth day of the Feast. It was incidentally the next day after the seven full weeks after the Passover, or the Day of Pentecost. On this gala occasion it was customary for the high priest to march through the crowded streets of the city in a grand procession to the pool of Siloam and to bring back a silver pitcher of water. While the procession moved dramatically through the streets the hopeful people sang joyously, "With joy shall ye draw water out of the wells of salvation" (Isaiah 12:3). Returning to the Temple court the priest reminded the people of the miraculous provision of water the Lord had made for their thirsty fathers in the wilderness as the result of Moses' striking the Rock. The water then was poured upon the brazen altar as a libation to the Lord.

As the grandiose and moving ceremony—purely of human origin—proceeded, the Priest also prophesied that as God had satisfied the physical thirst of the fathers in the wilderness a new day was coming when he would again visit them and slake their spiritual thirst according to the promises made through the prophets. But the priests seemed to know little of the time of such a visitation and even less of the Christ who then stood among them.

Present at this feast was Jesus and he took a special interest in the water ceremony. He saw the sham and emptiness of the priestly performers who went through their mechanical ritual with utter indifference to the fact that the Water of Life was in their midst. There was little comfort in their predictions of a coming day in which the people would receive living water. It served their mercenary purposes to preserve the status quo, to keep the people in spiritual darkness and to perpetuate themselves in office. Filled with contempt for the sacredotal imposters and touched with the feelings of the infirmities of the thirsty multitudes, Jesus cried out the good news that the day was near when every thirsty soul could be satisfied with the Water of Life, for the Holy Ghost was about to be given. He was about to be glorified and the Comforter would then come. Everything hinged upon accepting the invitation, "Come to me and drink," believing on Jesus, "as the Scripture hath said."

To the priests this was a stunning rebuke, but to the famishing and honest hearers it was the revival of hope. It was the voice of God, and they believed.

After his sojourn on earth as "God manifest in the flesh" he announced his purpose to depart and to return to his Father. Who could portray in language or art the infinitely blessed experiences the disciple had shared by having lived in his presence? How they had come to depend on him! In baffling situations—whether a stormy sea, an appearance before the conniving politicians, confrontation by death or devils, or facing starving multitudes with little or no bread on hand—they had come to regard Him as undisputed Master. He was indeed the Comforter. It is little wonder that sorrow filled their hearts upon hearing the announcement that He would go away. It was enough to have brought overwhelming bereavement to them, but see how he allayed their sorrow:

"And I will pray the Father, and he shall give you another Comforter, that he may abide with you forever; Even the Spirit of truth; whom the world cannot receive, because it seeth him not, neither knoweth him: but ye know him; for he dwelleth with you, and shall be in you. I will not leave you comfortless: I will come to you."

"At that day ye shall know that I am in my Father, and ye in me, and I in you. He that hath my commandments, and keepeth them, he it is that loveth me: and he that loveth me shall be loved of my Father, and I will love him, and will manifest myself to him."

"If a man love me, he will keep my words: and my Father will love him, and we will come unto him, and make our abode with him."

"But the Comforter, which is the Holy Ghost, whom the Father will send in my name, he shall teach you all things, and bring all things to your remembrance, whatsoever I have said unto you" (John 14:16-18, 20, 21, 23, 26).

"But when the Comforter is come, whom I will send unto you from the Father, even the Spirit of truth, which proceedeth from the Father, he shall testify of me: And ye also shall bear witness, because ye have been with me from the beginning" (John 15:26, 27).

"Nevertheless I tell you the truth; It is expedient for you that I go away: for if I go not away, the Comforter will not come unto you; but if I depart, I will send him unto you. And when he is come, he will reprove the world of sin, and of righteousness, and of judgment."

"I have yet many things to say unto you, but ye cannot bear them now. Howbeit when he, the Spirit of truth, is come, he will guide you into all truth: for he shall not speak of himself; but whatsoever he shall hear, that shall he speak: and he will shew you things to come" (John 16:7, 8, 12, 13).

These assuring promises, together with Jesus' explanation that it was "expedient"—beneficial—for them that He go away, assuaged their bereavement. They saw His going would be to their advantage, for in so doing He would send the Comforter, and that in a manner entirely mysterious to them, He would return to them, never again to depart. It was this assurance that they would not lose him that supplanted their grief. "I will not leave you comfortless: I will come to you," He had said. And with their eyes set on the world which needed evangelization, the coming of the Comforter would certainly be to their advantage because coming to them, "He would reprove (convince) the world of sin, and of righteousness, and of judgment," whereas if Jesus remained with them as they had known him in His localized person, He was limited to local situations, and consequently to a limited number.

It was expedient for them that Jesus should be exalted to the right hand of the Father, where, being equal with the Father, He could represent His people as their high priest and advocate. The disciples could, at least vaguely, see the wisdom of the urgency that He be exalted to the glory he had enjoyed with the Father before He came to be their Saviour. They began to realize too that it was urgent that they receive the "promise of the Father." It had become a "must." At the last meeting with them he had emphasized its imperativeness in the parting command, "Tarry ye in the city of Jerusalem, until ye be endued with power from on high" (Luke 24:49).

CHAPTER III

PENTECOST APPROACHING

THE Book of the Acts of the Apostles is introduced by Luke, the author, with a reference to the "Former treatise . . . of all that Jesus began to do and to teach," referring to his earlier work, the Gospel of Luke. Obviously the work of Jesus was interrupted momentarily by death that it might be resumed with accelerated force by a transference of the Spirit which was upon him to his followers. The Gospel of Luke simply introduced the story of Jesus, supplying a resume of His ministry in the flesh, of His resurrection and ascension. But that was not the end of His story. It is continued in the Book of Acts, which might well have been titled, "The Life of Jesus Christ Through the Power of the Holy Ghost." Or the title could have been "The Acts of the Holy Ghost" for it is only the Acts of the Apostles as they were agents of the Holy Ghost.

Luke provides for us a faint description of the last meeting of Jesus with the disciples before His ascension. The subject of their conversation was the promise of the Father. The record says:

"And, [Jesus] being assembled together with them, commanded them that they should not depart from Jerusalem, but wait for the promise of the Father, which, saith he, ye have heard of me. For John truly baptized with water; but ye shall be baptized with the Holy Ghost not many days hence" (Acts 1:4, 5).

Someone, still dreaming of a literal kingdom with Christ the King, and themselves administrators, attempted to change the subject, by injecting the question, "Wilt thou at this time restore again the kingdom to Israel?" But He quickly brought them back to the pertinent issue. His answer was a gentle rebuke to their ever ambitious hopes. Said he, "It is not for you to know the times or the seasons, which the Father hath put in his own power. But ye shall receive power, after that the Holy Ghost is come upon you" (Acts 1:6-8).

It is extraordinarily significant that the matter of the coming realization of the Promise of the Father, the coming of the Holy Ghost, should have been the topic of that last meeting. It had been the subject of his last message to them before His death. He had instructed them on the same subject during the forty days following the Resurrection. Could it be possible that He overemphasized its importance? Never! The future of the scheme of redemption depended upon their being endued with power from above. Without the power of the Holy Ghost Jesus knew the best of men would utterly fail and His cause would die aborning.

That was a glorious meeting. The disciples could never forget it. The impact of His last words to them would forever burn in their souls. Well they knew of the frailty of human character. How they must have blushed in His presence after His resurrection because of their cowardice, their breach of loyalty! His message had penetrated deeply into their hearts. Never again would they question His wisdom. They were ready to stop everything and "Tarry . . . until they were endued with power from on high." His work was done, "and a cloud received him out of their sight."

It was approximately ten days from the ascension of Jesus until the Day of Pentecost, but they have been called "The Ten Days That Changed the World." True to the Master's command the disciples were soon on their way to Jerusalem to await the fulfillment of the Promise, and "with great joy."

There is no note of sadness in the narrative of the ascension. No tears were shed unless they were tears of joy. A miracle had occurred. The disciples were convinced they had not lost Jesus. A greater miracle was about to happen, and they rejoiced in its anticipation.

The ten days of waiting have been called "The Long Pause." "We must again recall to mind that

most wonderful silence of ten days—that long, long pause of the Commissioned Church in sight of the perishing world. Never should the solemnity of that silence pass from the thoughts of any of God's people. It stands in the very forefront of our history—the Lord's most memorable and affecting protest beforehand—that no authority under heaven, that no training, that no ordination could qualify men to propagate the Gospel without the baptism of the Holy Ghost. Each successive day of those solemn and silent ten, the perishing world might have knocked at the door of the Church, and asked, 'What waitest thou for, O bride of the ascended Bridegroom? Why dost thou not say, "Come"? Why leavest thou us to slumber on uncalled, unwarned, unblessed, whilst thou, with thy good tidings, art tarrying inactive there? What waitest thou for?' and every moment the answer would have been, 'We are waiting to be "endued with power from on high"; we are waiting to be "baptized with the Holy Ghost and fire." ' "
—*The Tongue of Fire*, by William Arthur, M.A., 1880.

This is the explanation of what the disciples did in the interim: "And were continually in the temple, praising and blessing God. Amen" (Luke 24:53).

CHAPTER IV

PENTECOST FULLY COME

W HEN the day of Pentecost was fully come" are the opening words of the second chapter of the Acts, serving as introductory words to a new era, marking the end of long ages of hopes deferred, languishings and vigils for the appearance of a God good enough and great enough to meet the needs of men everywhere. In Jesus the relatively few who came to know Him recognized that He was sufficient goodness, and that He was absolute master in any situation when present. But the world was so vast that no one expected Him to heal broken hearts and calm troubled souls in every far away place. "Pentecost fully come"—the great Pentecost of which all previous Feasts of Pentecost were only types or shadows—meant the dawning of an era in which Jesus Christ would no longer be restricted, hampered or limited in a corporeal body as in the days of the flesh, but it meant that He would be released into all the world to become a universal, omnipresent personality through the gift of the Holy Ghost. Thus

41

He would henceforth be equally within reach of all men.

Pentecost was the fiftieth day after the Passover. Fifty days after the first Passover God had given the Law to Israel. The sight was a majestic and awesome one which would never be forgotten. While Israel encamped at the base of Mt. Sinai, Moses climbed to its height to meet the God of Israel. The mountain was shrouded in eerie blackness, darkness, tempest and was burning with fire, while a frightening, trumpet-like voice enunciated the immutable, inexorable terms of God's holy Covenant. "And so terrible was the sight, that Moses said, I exceedingly fear and quake" (Hebrews 12:18-21). This was the first Pentecost.

"Pentecost fully come" was fifty days after "Christ our Passover" was "sacrificed for us" (1 Corinthians 5:7). This was the day God would seal the New Covenant with a baptism of Fire. The sight again is majestic and awesome as is every manifestation of the holy God, but it is not fearful, because, "Ye are not come unto the mount that might be touched, and that burned with fire, nor unto blackness, and darkness, and tempest, And the sound of a trumpet, and the voice of words; which voice they that heard intreated that the word should not be spoken to them any more . . . But ye are come unto mount Sion . . . And to Jesus the mediator of the new covenant, and to the blood of sprinkling, that speaketh better things than that of Abel" (Hebrews 12:18-24).

The tenor of this meeting of the apostles was "joy unspeakable and full of glory," the kind of bliss to be found where hearts are of one accord. There was no bemoaning their absent Lord. The old strife of "who should be greatest in the kingdom" was gone, and there was no note of doubt or rivalry. The "ten days that changed the world" had first wrought a remarkable change in the hitherto carnal, ambitious disciples. About one hundred twenty men and women were present, and "they were all of one accord." All the disciples were present, including Thomas. No one was late. In fact they seem to have arrived quite early, for it was only about nine o'clock in the morning when Peter began to preach.

No one knew how long the tarrying would continue, but they had reached the point of no return and no one would go back until they received the Promise from the Father. They had arrived at the place of losing themselves in the worship of God, "and were continually . . . praising and blessing God." This is an example of the proper frame of mind and the depth of consecration requisite to receiving the gift of the Holy Ghost.

"And suddenly there came a sound from heaven as of a rushing mighty wind, and it filled all the house where they were sitting. And there appeared unto them cloven tongues like as of fire, and it sat upon each of them. And they were all filled with the Holy Ghost, and began to speak with other tongues, as the Spirit gave them utterance" (Acts 2:2-4).

Contemplate the supernatural manifestations that accompanied the advent of the Holy Ghost: the Sound from Heaven, the Celestial Fire, Speaking with other Tongues.

The Sound From Heaven

The sound from heaven came suddenly and unexpectedly. To the disciples it sounded like a mighty rushing wind, but it was not wind. It was not like a sudden squall that shook the house from without. There was nothing to indicate that the wind was astir. The air in the room where the disciples were waiting was as calm as usual, but they heard a sound like a hurricane, and all agreed that it came—not from an open door or window—but downward from heaven. The Greek word for Spirit is *Pneuma*, and means breath, air or wind. This was the breath of God upon the waiting disciples.

The Celestial Fire

Cloven tongues of fire sat upon each brow. It was not an ordinary physical fire as we know it, for it did no damage. It too was from heaven. It came in fulfillment of the prediction of John the Baptist who said of Jesus, "He shall baptize you with the Holy

Ghost and with fire." It was not a shapeless flame of fire, but in each case the appearance was as of cloven tongues. It was symbolic of the power with which the church was to be endowed, for which they had waited and prayed, and by which they would be enabled to bear witness unto the risen Christ "unto the uttermost part of the earth." The cloven tongue appeared on each, so that each one had the fire-impulse to go and to tell the message of reconciliation.

Adorning each brow of the one hundred twenty present, the fire was a symbol of the end of the old regime. Contrary to accepted custom, women and commoners were now entering the realm of life previously inhabited by a small minority of priests and prophets. The ancient system with its endless ceremonies of formal worship was waxing old and was ready to vanish. Every individual from the least to the greatest might now know God. The time had arrived when all might worship the Father in the Spirit. The proud, Christ-rejecting priesthood might yet kindle fires on the brazen altar, but the heavenly fire had gone out there, and God was as the symbol denoting transferring it to the Church. "They shall say no more, The ark of the covenant of the Lord: neither shall it come to mind: neither shall they remember it; neither shall they visit it; neither shall that be done any more" (Jeremiah 3:16).

It was the reception of this power, of which the cloven tongues was the symbol, for which our Lord commanded the disciples to wait, and for which all other operations were to stand still. How significant! How arrogant of men to invade the sacred precincts of divine appointment without having waited for this power, which the Head of the Church deemed so imperative.

Speaking With Other Tongues

Volumes have been written on this subject, pro and con, but it remains part of the record. The fact of the peculiar phenomenon of speaking with other tongues certainly had not been anticipated by the disciples when they went to the meeting. This adds to the mystery of it.

As we have previously explained the time was the Feast of Pentecost. A tremendous crowd was present in Jerusalem, for the Feast was somewhat of a Jewish world fair. It is said that not less than two million strangers were often in attendance in and around their sacred city celebrating the Feast. What a fitting time for "Pentecost fully come" and the heavenly visitation with signs and wonders! The sound from heaven and the celestial fire had been witnessed, as far as we know, only by the one hundred twenty. The sign of speaking in other languages by supernatural utterance, though it began while no one else was present, was designed to make it possible for those of every nation represented to hear the gospel in his native tongue. The record is quite clear that "they began to speak with other tongues," before the multitude came together, which lends credence to the belief, particularly in view of the other similar experiences recorded in the Book of Acts, that it was initially a personal evidence of the baptism of the Holy Ghost.

It was the astonishment of hearing the unlearned Galileans speak fluently in languages unknown to them that overwhelmingly dumbfounded the multitudes. "How hear we every man in his own tongue?" "What meaneth this?" they asked. The answers varied according to the spiritual perception of the hearers. "The wonderful works of God," some exclaimed. Others protested, "These men are full of new wine."

The narrator has not told us what the Spirit-filled disciples were saying in their newly acquired gifts of speech, but unquestionably it was the "good news" of the crucified and risen Saviour, exalted at the right hand of the Father, mysteriously manifesting his universal presence in the miracles of that day. And what a privilege it was for the delegates from all over the known world to hear the gospel in their own languages superhumanly spoken.

The climax of the happenings of this historic day was not the accompanying signs of wind, fire and the physical manifestation of speaking with tongues, but the glorious fact that "They were all filled with the Holy Ghost." Jesus had said, "Ye shall be baptized with the Holy Ghost not many days hence," and it was now a reality. (Technically there is a difference between being "filled with the Holy Ghost" and being "baptized with the Holy Ghost." One may not be baptized with the Holy Ghost without also being filled with the Holy Ghost, although he may be filled with the Spirit again and again.) It meant that Jesus at the right hand of the Father had prayed for them and that the Comforter had arrived. It also meant that in that experience Jesus had come to them. They knew that He was in the Father and in them and that they were in Him. This was the manner in which He though now invisible had promised to "manifest" himself to them. Father, Son and Holy Ghost were now all resident in the believers (John 14:16-26). The Church which is his body, and the habitation of God through the Spirit was born, and was a living, vibrant entity. Small and embryonic, the church possessing the Spirit of life, was capable of perpetuating itself and was destined to fill the earth. The gates of hell would never prevail against it.

In a drama of the *Trial of Jesus* by John Mansfield there is an interview between the Roman centurion who was responsible for the execution of Jesus, and Pilate's wife Procula. In the interview Procula quizzed him concerning the death of Jesus. She inquired how he died. Then she asked, "Do you think he is dead?"

"No," he replied.

"Then where is he?"

"Let loose in the world, Lady," he continued, "where neither Roman nor Jew can stop his truth." True indeed. Jesus is the Eternal Contemporary because of the miracle of Pentecost. Thus is his own word verified, "Lo, I am with you alway, even unto the end of the world."

The First Pentecostal Sermon

The new-born church found its voice at Pentecost. It was born with a message. If prior to that day the disciples were afraid to speak, having received the Holy Ghost they could not refrain. Out of the experience of Pentecost they had gained a message.

The first sermon of the New Testament Church was delivered by Peter, much to the surprise of those who may have recalled his cowardly breach of allegiance to the Lord on the night of His betrayal. That had been fifty days ago and after the Resurrection he had seen the Lord and everything had been fixed with Him, and Peter had humbly gone along with the others to tarry for the Holy Ghost. And the sermon—although extemporaneous—was highly intelligent, expository, complete, powerfully provocative and boldly delivered. There were three points to it:

I. *This is that spoken by the Prophet Joel.*

The days the prophets promised have come.

The new era has dawned. This was fulfillment of Joel's prophecy: "This is that which was spoken by the prophet Joel; And it shall come to pass in the last days, saith God, I will pour out of my Spirit upon all flesh: and your sons and your daughters . . . your young men . . . your old men . . . my servants . . . and on my handmaidens . . ." (Acts 2:15-21).

II. *Jesus of Nazareth, crucified, resurrected and exalted, is Christ.*

The same Jesus crucified is now risen and at the right hand of God. The events of the day were definitely connected with the promise of Jesus as well as that of Joel and David. These facts establish His claims to be the "anointed of God." It is He that "hath shed forth this, which ye now see and hear" (Acts 2:33).

III. *Since these things are true, repentance is in Order.*

"Repent, and be baptized every one of you in the name of Jesus Christ for the remission of sins, and ye shall receive the gift of the Holy Ghost" (Acts 2:38).

Pentecost brought about, at least in one man, a supersensory understanding. It brought a new insight into the Scriptures. Peter's sermon was a masterpiece of Old Testament exposition. From the standpoint of arrangement it was superb, and for results it was without parallel. But we are amazed when we discover that it had not been planned by Peter. There is no proof that Peter was in charge of the meeting. He did not know what to expect when he attended that morning meeting. It is most unlikely that he was expected to speak, or even that he anticipated doing so. Yet he arose on the spur of the moment and spoke coherently, boldly and clearly. One wonders how he so readily opened up the meaning of the passages from the Book of Joel and from the Psalms, and indeed how he knew what they meant, when without the light he has shed on them, we might be less certain of their interpretation. But there is an explanation: Peter was filled with the Holy Ghost.

If the Jews were to be convinced of the claims of Christ, it would certainly have to be by their own Scriptures. They would have to be convinced that it was none other than Jesus of Nazareth to whom the Scriptures pointed. Thus every statement of that sermon was based on Jewish Scripture. The Holy Spirit enabled Peter to see in the Scriptures significances never before expressed. The Scriptures are Spirit inspired, and the Spirit is their best interpreter.

After many weary hours of teaching precious truths to the dull minds of fishermen and publicans, Jesus told them: "I have yet many things to say unto you, but ye cannot bear them now. Howbeit when he, the Spirit of truth, is come, he will guide you into all truth: for he shall not speak of himself; but whatsoever he shall hear, that shall he speak: and he will shew you things to come" (John 16:12-15). The Spirit, also known as the Spirit of Truth, had come, and in a flash of inner illumination he had taught Peter what he might otherwise have never learned.

CHAPTER V

THE CROSS AND PENTECOST

THE disciples of Jesus entertained great hopes of an immediate revolution that would either by force or by miracle overthrow their Roman masters and restore the kingdom to Israel under a glorious leadership which they were certain Jesus would provide. This was a cherished belief among the Israelites and was what they expected of the Messiah. It was also the dream of the disciples as is revealed again and again in reference to the constant strife among them that continued almost to the time of the death of Jesus; i.e., "Who shall be greatest in the Kingdom?" It seemed almost impossible for the truth of His purpose concerning the Kingdom to penetrate their understanding, so that at last he abruptly shattered their dream by telling them, "It is not for you to know the times nor the seasons which the Father hath put in his own power." This was in answer to their question, "Wilt thou at this time restore the Kingdom to Israel?" And it was on the day of His ascension.

Nevertheless Jesus' plans were clear. He had come to the world, not primarily to become the world's greatest teacher or miracle worker, or an earthly monarch, but to become the Lamb of God—the Lamb slain from the foundation of the world—and by a vicarious death to bear away the sins of the world. From the day of His birth the cross had cast an ugly shadow across His pathway. He was not unmindful of its meaning. He entered officially into His ministry fully aware of all it meant. It was no surprise to Him that He lived in the shadow of the cross and that He was en route to Calvary from the day He left the ivory palaces and came to earth.

The disciples also lived in that shadow. They believed He was the Christ, but something very mysterious enveloped Him which was beyond their comprehension. Some of His sayings mystified them to the point of bewilderment. For example, Jesus once said, "As Moses lifted up the serpent in the wilderness, even so must the Son of man be lifted up" (John 3:14). This was said early in His ministry. Much later he said, "And I, if I be lifted up from the earth, will draw all men unto me" (John 12:32, 33). We know now that both these passages were spoken with reference to His death; but they were dark sayings to them. Then immediately after that blessed time when he had asked that poignant question, "Whom say ye that I am?" and Peter had responded so enthusiastically, the Son of God, Jesus followed by announcing, "The Son of man must suffer many things, and be rejected of the elders and chief priests and scribes, and be slain, and be raised the third day" (Luke 9:22). Yes, He knew about the cross, and while His words terrified the disciples they were unable to acquiesce to a cross in the life of their victorious Messiah. This is clear by the reaction of Peter, who "took him, and began to rebuke him, saying, Be it far from thee, Lord: this shall not be unto thee" (Matthew 16:22). No doubt Peter expressed the sentiment of the others.

It was because they lived in the shadowland that it was so difficult for them to believe. They were trying to understand, but His words fell upon dull ears. Though they were objects of His most anxious care and what was spoken to others in parables was explained to them in the most literal simplicity, they, nevertheless, remained incapable of comprehending Him. It was not unwillingness on their part that hindered, but incapacity. Their unbelief was not willful, and Jesus understood. They were utterly dumbfounded when Jesus girded Himself with a towel and washed their feet. His words to them on that occasion were calculated to put their minds at ease. "What I do thou knowest not now"; He said, "but thou shalt know hereafter" (John 13:7, 8). They did not understand the simple parable of defilement, and when Peter asked that he declare it unto them, he answered as if he were weary, "Are ye also yet without understanding?" (Matthew 15:16). Almost at the very end of their course of training under the greatest Teacher it appeared that they had not learned the basic lessons well, for we find Philip saying at the Last Supper, "Lord, shew us the Father, and it sufficeth us." Patiently Jesus responded, "Have I been so long time with you, and yet hast thou not known me, Philip?" (John 14:8, 9). But Jesus did not give up. Patiently He labored with an assurance that by and by His words would become known. What was falling upon dull ears was not lost. Like seed sown and lost in the dark soil, His word would be quick and alive. Hopefully He restated and amplified the promise again the same evening: "I have many things to say unto you, but ye cannot bear them now. Howbeit when he, the Spirit of truth, is come, he will guide you into all truth" (John 16:12, 13). In a few hours Jesus was hanging on the cross. The shadows were very real. But He had done His work well; He had given them the Father's word, and though they might appear then to be lost, the Spirit of Truth would quicken their memory and bring back whatsoever Jesus had said unto them. The day was dark indeed, but there was the promise of a day when the mysteries would clear away like clouds before the sun.

When did the disciples emerge from the shadows and learn of the victory of the cross? They did not learn at the cross, nor at the resurrection. The resurrection found them hiding behind barred doors for fear of the Jews. Never was there a more defeated or dejected group. They knew they were not victorious even after they had seen the Lord alive. Even then Peter had gone back to his nets and to the fishing business, being joined by others of their company. This is most significant. Bear in mind that all the facts of redemption according to the prophecies were complete. The Lamb of God had been slain, the atoning blood had been shed, the vicarious sacrifice had been approved. The resurrection was the certification of that fact. He was resurrected for our justification. The price was paid in full for the redemption of all mankind. But no one was being saved. There was no revival. No one proclaimed the good news of the finished work of Calvary. There is no record of the conversion of a single soul between the day of the crucifixion and the day of Pentecost. Yet they had received the Great Commission. How may we account for the calm, listless, apathetic inertia of the disciples? Why the cessation of activity when the world was so much in need of the gospel?

The answer is obvious? The job ahead was so stupendous that they dared not tackle it without "power from on high." Jesus had not relied upon His death to inspire them, or His resurrection to convince them, or the ascension to open their eyes. He had told them in no uncertain terms of "the promise of the Father," and commanded them to "Tarry . . . until they be endued with power from on high." Without

a confirmed ministry—one approved supernaturally
—they realized now they were incompetent. Thus
until the day come when they should receive the
"power of the Holy Ghost" the great Captain of our
Salvation ordered that all business be suspended, that
all operations stand still, and that the whole world
wait.

Then the great day came! It was just fifty days
after the Passover-crucifixion. It was the Day of
Pentecost, true to the type. It was the one to which
all other Pentecosts had pointed. With it there came
the triumph of a cause most people deemed hope-
lessly lost. The Church was suddenly alive with a
hitherto unknown passion. It ceased hiding behind
barred doors. It had a story to tell, and was telling
it openly and aggressively. The revival started that
day. Three thousand were converted and baptized.
The victory of Pentecost proved to be the victory of
the Cross. The victory the Church enjoyed at Pentecost and forever after was won at Calvary.

One of the objections to the doctrine of the baptism of the Holy Ghost, is allegedly, that Pentecostals
make it a "plus to Calvary," an addition to the finished work of the cross. This should never be the
case. The great purpose of Pentecost is to turn the
floodlights on Calvary. If there had been no Passover there could have been no Pentecost. Pentecost is
pointless without the message of the Cross. The work
of the Lord at Pentecost was the complement of the

work of the cross, for it was the feast of the Lord showing the results of the dying of Christ, our Passover, as represented by the two loaves (see Feast of Pentecost in chapter 1). The Passover represents the "corn of wheat" that fell into the earth and died; Pentecost, the result of its dying and "bringeth forth much fruit" (John 12:24). It is apparent that Pentecost cannot be divorced from Calvary, and vice versa. This is the practical lesson that may be readily seen by referring to Acts 2. The new power that clothed the Church was the ability to proclaim and publish the story of Jesus Christ, crucified, resurrected and exalted to the right hand of the Father. This was the purpose of the coming of the Comforter according to Jesus, who said, "He shall testify of me" (John 15:26).

The coming of the Comforter indeed cleared up the shadows. The mysteries they had been unable to penetrate disappeared, and they suddenly understood the meaning of the cross. A supersensory understanding, an inner revelation, was theirs. The hard sayings of the Master which had baffled their dull minds now plainly fell into place like the pieces of a jigsaw puzzle. Even the cross and the agonies of the Lord, which had caused them to lose hope fifty days ago, were now for the first time visibly clear. They were ready to proclaim that story to the world, beginning right in the city of Jerusalem where they had suffered their most humiliating defeat. They would confront the rulers of Israel with their story. And whereas they had hidden themselves for fear of the Jews, that fear also had mysteriously vanished. They would turn the world upside down with their message. "Pentecost made a difference between weakness, fear, timidity, and joyous daring."—E. Stanley Jones.

It is at Calvary's cross and there alone that sinners may be reconciled to God and find eternal life. But the "Go ye" that drives men and women to the ends of the earth as living sacrifices to make that message known begins at Pentecost.

CHAPTER VI

PENTECOSTAL REVOLUTION

PENTECOST proved to be a veritable revolution in the history of Israel, in the despised, insignificant disciples of Jesus, and in the lives of individual believers. The impact of Pentecost as a force that was destined to make history was manifestly at work. With the outpouring of the Holy Ghost the followers of Jesus began to be recognized as the Church, to which, as the revival fires spread, the Lord was adding substantial numbers daily. On the contrary, having rejected their Messiah and having crucified their King, Israel's sun was rapidly sinking. Their violent protests and persecutions against the vigorous young Church were the death struggles of a system from which the glory had departed. Israel was retreating before the invincible march of the Church against which the gates of hell shall not prevail.

In the wake of the mighty move of the Holy Ghost personalities were revolutionized. So-called revivals or awakenings that do not change individuals are anomalous to the Pentecostal pattern. They make little impact on society. The change in the disciples was dynamic and revolutionary.

The pre-Pentecostal picture of the disciples of Christ is certainly not a gratifying one. Aside from the fact that they had been chosen by our Lord, that their names were in heaven, that they were clean through the Word he had spoken unto them, and that he had prayed for them, there is little in their lives to provoke us to emulation. Despite their close association with Jesus they were a very carnal, proud, selfish, sectarian, conniving, cowardly, ambitious, vindicative group. Because of their warped, unwarranted imaginations about the coming Kingdom, they carried on a running battle over who should be the greatest in the Kingdom. Feelings ran high and were hotly expressed. It is very likely that Peter aspired to the position of prime minister of the Messianic kingdom, and just as probable that James and John were his rivals. This reprehensible rivalry brought forth from Jesus the tactful reproof so adroitly administered by calling a little child unto Him and commenting, poignantly, "Except ye be converted, and become as little children, ye shall not enter into the kingdom of heaven" (Matthew 18:1-5). This state of affairs, sometimes reaching proportions of a political dispute, continued until Jesus was within only a few hours of the cross.

There were times when the disciples manifested an attitude wholly foreign to the spirit of Jesus. For example: Rebuffed at a village of Samaria because it did not accept the offer of Jesus to visit there, James and John—appropriately named "Sons of Thunder"—proposed calling fire down from heaven to consume the village.

The disciples were often at variance with the purposes of Jesus because they were unable to evaluate or to appreciate them. Impatient with the milling multitudes and unable to share His compassion for them, they besought the Master to send them away with no thought that many of them might faint along the way, for the hour was late and they had followed Him far from home. They became very indignant at Mary's lavish ado in wasting the costly ointment to anoint her Lord. They were outraged when they discovered someone casting out devils in the name of Jesus, because he was not of their company, and they summarily restrained him. But Jesus rebuked their sectarianism, saying, "Forbid him not." Peter demonstrated his own pitiable lack of spiritual depth when he presumed to rebuke the Lord. This defection was followed by his shameful denial of and forsaking of Jesus. At one point the Scripture relates that they all forsook Him and fled. When Jesus was buried all their faith and hopes were buried with Him. They lapsed into a state of harassing fear. In their indescribable despair they hid behind barred doors. Only a dynamic revolution could bring them out.

But Pentecost was a dynamic revolution. It made a difference. Suddenly they were out of hiding. Openly they declared the gospel story. Weakness, fear and timidity gave way to dauntless courage. Fearlessly they preached Christ crucified and resurrected to the city that had put Him to death. They publicly confronted their rulers and charged them with His murder. The revolution so pronounced of the corporate group was the composite of individual revolutions. What happened to the group had been experienced individually.[1]

Everyone present on the Day of Pentecost experienced a blessed revolution. The experience of Peter is a vivid example. How changed he was! He lost sight of his cherished ambition to be the greatest in the Kingdom. The rivalry with his brethren was gone. He was cured of his vacillating cowardice. It was he who delivered the first sermon of the church, and that in a hostile community. Before the councils and courts he was intrepid, eloquent, magnanimous, radiant and gentle. At last he had drunk deeply of the

---

1. Contrary to the view that the baptism of the Holy Ghost was a sovereign act on the part of God by which He baptized the church once and for all time, the simple truth is that He baptized and continues to baptize each individual severally. Yet that position contains a semblance of truth, for the coming of the Holy Ghost was given for the entire church age. It is not necessary for anyone to plead for God to again send the Comforter. He is come. It does not therefore follow that every individual in the church is automatically baptized with the Holy Ghost. Christ tasted death for every man, yet all agree that not every man is saved. God respects the free will of man and personal salvation depends upon personal, individual response to the gospel proposition. The same is true concerning the Holy Ghost baptism, as the Book of Acts verifies. See Acts 2:4; 9:17; 10:44-48; 19:2-6.

spirit of Jesus. He was the same man, but Peter was filled with the Holy Ghost.

The other disciples were likewise Spirit-filled and marvelously revolutionized. The Holy Ghost baptism is a personality gift. Christ baptizes personalities. He only baptizes individuals, not organizations, systems, or methods. The sphere of the Spirit is consecrated men—individual temples. In receiving the Spirit men receive "The Spirit of power, and of love, and of a sound mind" (2 Timothy 1:7). To be most like Jesus men must imbibe of His Spirit; must share the same Baptism He received. Man at his best is man filled with the Holy Ghost.

It was in the Pentecostal blessing that Jesus transferred to the Church the power that had rested upon Him. It was in this manner that he "received of the Father the promise of the Holy Ghost," as mentioned by Peter in the first Pentecostal sermon (Acts 2:33). It was the realization of the Father's promise to the Son that the Holy Ghost should be "shed forth" upon the Church.

The Sacredotal System Loses Priority

The Pentecostal revolution wrought havoc with the status quo which favored the few who claimed theocratic privilege and precedence. It disrupted deep-rooted traditions, which because of their antiquity were regarded as commandments of God. It upset those who proudly imagined that because of

their temple monoply that the God of the universe
would be compelled to use their ecclesiastical machinery in order to do business with the world. They
boasted ostentatiously that they were the children of
Abraham, as though that relieved them of further
moral responsibility. Enamored of their own glory
and wisdom they could not see the infinite wisdom
of God revealed in His only begotten Son. Therefore,
the long-awaited refreshing of which the prophets
had told came, not to the Temple, but to an upper
room of a private residence. It bypassed the arrogant priesthood, so satisfied, so able and mature with
worldly wisdom. This was an imperceptable tragedy!
Who could describe it?

To be sure they carried on for a few decades. They
continued their anemic form of worship. Crowds still
came, though throngs had gone with the Church.
They continued their sacrifices, but they were meaningless. The Great Sacrifice of which theirs were
only shadows had now been offered. "Ichabod" might
well have been posted above their altars, for indeed
the glory had departed. The fire from heaven had
eclipsed the altar fires and settled within the church
which Jesus said he would build. There was little
need now to light a candle; the Sun of Righteousness was shining in full orbed glory.

There would never be again a legitimate mediatory
priesthood which would halt the true worshiper at
the Temple gate saying, "Thus far and no farther.

You must have an earthly mediator to represent you before God." Since Pentecost every believer is a priest, with access to the Holy of Holies through the Spirit. "Ye are a royal priesthood" (1 Peter 2:9). "And hast made us unto our God kings and priests" (Revelation 5:10). "There is one mediator between God and men, the man Christ Jesus" (1 Timothy 2:5). Through him all have equal rights and access unto the Father.

Sacred Shrines Displaced

In conformity with the Pentecostal revolution there at once ceased to be the necessity of sacred shrines and holy places. Seekers for God no longer must go to Jerusalem, Mt. Gerizim, Mecca, or the Ganges River, or to any other hallowed spot. God had long been seeking for worshipers who would worship Him in spirit. He had planned a time when "Spirit with spirit would commune." The time had come. Now God could be found everywhere. The wonderful personality of Jesus Christ was diffused into the world through the power of the Holy Ghost. Now the commonest place on earth may be a shrine. The poor, the unfortunate, the isolated may as truly worship God in the Holy Ghost by his own humble hearth as he could in the Temple at Jerusalem. In a few short years not one stone of the magnificent Temple in Jerusalem would be left upon another, but the true worshiper would continue to worship his God in the

Spirit, because every believer is a "Temple of the Holy Ghost."

Class Barriers Collapse

The social status, long in need of redemption, could not escape the impact of the Pentecostal Revolution. Though unwritten as law custom had crystalized into a class distinction as adamant as that of the Indian caste system. But the coming of the Holy Ghost disregarded all racial and class barriers. "He hath made of one blood all nations." The ground is all level at the Cross. There are those who labor tirelessly to rebuild the old partitions, but they labor in vain. They are down forever. The Pentecostal outpouring very soon overflowed national barriers, and Gentiles were ushered in to the household of faith. The days of Israel's sacred monopoly were over.

By a most unique coincidence shortly after Pentecost we find Peter a guest in the house of Simon, a tanner in Joppa. Tanning was an unclean business. To come into contact with one engaged in so unclean a business was ceremonial defilement. And Peter was a man of scruples. From the tenor of the narrative it appears that Peter was ill at ease and uncertain as to whether he should eat with Simon and his family. He therefore remained fasting and praying on the housetop, although he was quite hungry. God knew the earnestness of his heart and answered his prayer by letting down a sheet filled with a variety of clean and unclean animals, and straightway commanded Peter to "slay and eat." Peter was shocked and registered the objection that he had never eaten anything common or unclean, but his objection was categorically overruled thus: "What God has cleansed call not thou common." The message was effective and Peter understood by it that the gospel was for all, and that he must withhold it from no one. The feeling of belonging to a superrace was gone—at least for the time—and Simon Peter was soon on his way to Caesarea to preach to Gentiles, an act so revolutionary that it shook both Jews and Gentiles.

In God's new creation "there is no room for Greek and Jew, circumcised and uncircumcised, barbarian, Scythian, slave, or free man; Christ is everything and everywhere" (Colossians 3:11, Moffatt). This is the "kingdom" of "righteousness, peace and joy in the Holy Ghost" (Romans 14:17).

Ceremonialism Revolutionized

The unique manner in which the Holy Ghost came upon the waiting disciples on the Day of Pentecost in utter disregard of the orthodox and complex ceremonialism pre-scheduled to take care of any and all divine manifestations is highly significant. If those ceremonies were "means of grace," the manner in which the Holy Ghost came eloquently declared that they had waxed old and had vanished away. Like antiquated electric wiring, they were inadequate for the high voltage of the Holy Ghost. Here was a divine innovation with far-reaching consequences. Henceforth the manifestation of the Spirit of God would not be under the control of a human system of ceremonialism.

It was never intended that Christian worship should be reduced to a ritualistic form. God is too great to be demonstrated by human inventions or by fixed aesthetic ceremony. In deference to the wisdom of the Holy Spirit New Testament writers have offered us no concrete form of service. Only two sacraments are handed down to us from the Apostles —Christian baptism and the Lord's Supper. (The latter ceremony includes the washing of feet.) But no fixed form for these is offered in the New Testament.

There have arisen beautiful and impressive ceremonies for every phase of worship, but when the Holy Ghost chooses to manifest himself, he sets them all aside. Man can no more build a channel to contain and govern the Spirit than he can control the tides. The great fault with ceremonialism is that the planners could not always anticipate the mind of the Spirit. They leave no place for his manifestation. It is presumptuous to suppose he must conform to a fixed form. There are instances where the omniscient Spirit chooses to manifest himself in a way for which no ceremonial provision has been made. At least on one occasion an apostolic sermon was interrupted by the coming of the Holy Ghost upon the congregation. No objection was offered, however, by either the apostle or the congregation. The wisdom of God had prevailed. The results were far more effective than the completed sermon of the great apostle might have been. The grand objective of the gospel was realized. The gift of the Holy Ghost upon the eager listeners was God's confirmation of the words of Peter (Acts 10:44-48).

Much ceremonial worship of today is perfunctory, but quite in order, because it is not expected that the Holy Ghost should come. Ceremonies are quite convenient and necessary in his absence. But He wants to come. Jesus desires to manifest himself to us through the Spirit (John 14:21). God forbid that our staid prearrangements and programing be allowed to shut Him out.

"Ritualism, like eczema in the human body, is generally a symptom of a low estate of the blood. As a rule, when the church becomes secularized, it becomes ritualized, while great revivals, p o u r i n g through the church have almost always burst the liturgical bands and have restored it to freedom of the Spirit."—Dr. A. J. Gordon.

Communities Revolutionized

A glowing example of the impact of the full gospel message upon a pagan community is furnished us in the incident of Paul's ministry in the city of Ephesus. Ephesus was a great metropolis, center of wealth and culture, but its people were chiefly worshipers of the goddess Diana, reputed to have fallen from heaven as a gift from Jupiter. Into that imposing stronghold of Satan came the insignificant little Jewish-Christian missionary, separated to the work of God, called, sent forth by and aflame with the Holy Ghost.

Upon his arrival in Ephesus he found a small band of believers, disciples of Apollos, an Alexandrian Jew, who knew and preached only the baptism of John, though he was learned, mighty in the Scriptures, eloquent and very zealous. A very excellent combination. However, Apollos had not learned of the crucifixion, resurrection and ascension of Jesus, nor of the advent of the Holy Ghost. To the little band of believers Paul asked, "Have ye received the Holy Ghost since ye believed?" Learning that they had not heard about the Holy Ghost, especially the Pentecostal outpouring, Paul introduced them to Christian baptism in the name of the Lord Jesus. Then he laid his hands on them and prayed for them. Immediately "the Holy Ghost came on them; and they spake with tongues, and prophesied" (Acts 19:1-7).

This was the beginning of a glorious awakening, which spread like a prairie fire throughout the city and throughout Asia Minor, and continued for three years (Acts 20:31). It was so effective that it so completely transformed the way of life of those converted from idolatry and sorcery that many of them brought their books of "curious arts," of magic and black art—and in joyful proclamation of their faith in Christ Jesus the Saviour, they publicly burned them. Fifty thousand pieces of silver was the estimated value of the bonfire, but it was a magnificent testimony of the power of the gospel and that the believers had made a clean and permanent break with the past.

The revolution was so pronounced and so sweeping that "there arose no small stir about that way. For a certain man named Demetrius, a silversmith, which made silver shrines for Diana, brought no small gain unto the craftsmen; Whom he called together with the workmen of like occupation, and said, Sirs, ye know that by this craft we have our wealth. Moreover ye see and hear, that not alone at Ephesus, but almost throughout all Asia, this Paul hath persuaded and turned away much people, saying that they be no gods, which are made with hands: So that not only this our craft is in danger to be set at nought; but also that the temple of the great goddess Diana should be despised, and her magnificence should be destroyed, whom all Asia and the world worshippeth" (Acts 19:23-27).

Revolution consistently follows in the wake of the Pentecostal revival in every age and every land. Pentecostal revival means revolution.

CHAPTER VII

PENTECOSTAL FIRE

F IRE has from time immemorial been associated with the worship of God. It has been recognized as a symbol of God by pagans, Jews and Christians.

In ancient Rome fire was kept burning simultaneously on a thousand altars. When that fire went out, we are told, all business of the State ceased. When the fire goes out in the Church its business is paralyzed. A fireless altar is the sad picture of rejection. It means the temple has lost its God, and that such a temple is no longer an acceptable place of worship. It means also that the worshiper is not acceptable before his God.

Isaiah referred to the indescribable Majesty as the "Devouring Fire," and the "Everlasting Burnings" (33:14, 15). "The glory of the Lord was like devouring fire on the top of the mount" (Exodus 24:17). Yet Moses went into that fire and was not consumed, though "Our God is a consuming fire" (Hebrews 12:29).

It was by fire that the invisible God chose to reveal himself on numerous occasions in Old Testament history. It was by fire that He first revealed
Himself to Moses. By the pillar of cloud and fire He
led the children of Israel through the wilderness. He
was reputed as "The God that answereth by fire."
Thus did Elijah the Tishbite challenge the prophets of
Baal, "The God that answereth by fire, let him be
God" (1 Kings 18:24).

Fire of supernatural origin has appeared on the altars of acceptable worshipers since the first penitent
man learned to worship God. Its presence was ever
a token of divine acceptance, and its absence a sign
of certain rejection. Thus did God distinguish between the sacrifices of Cain and Abel. To Cain in his
jealous wrath, God remonstrated, "If thou doest well
shalt thou not be accepted?"

When the priests of Israel began their ministry,
having prepared the brazen altar and the sacrifices
according to specifications given to Moses, "The
glory of the Lord appeared unto all the people. And
there came a fire out from before the Lord, and consumed upon the altar the burnt offering and the fat"
(Leviticus 9:23, 24). It was the responsibility of
the priests thereafter to keep the holy fire burning.
"And the fire upon the altar shall be burning in it;
it shall not be put out . . . The fire shall ever be
burning upon the altar; it shall never go out" (Leviticus 6:12, 13).

This is a beautiful and impressive symbol of the coming of God's Spirit and of our responsibility to live in such a manner that He shall not be grieved, offended and consequently take his departure from us. Recall the prayer of David, "Take not thy Holy Spirit from me."

Thus fire became a symbol of the presence of the holy God expressing himself, and in manifestation of that which he approved. Israel learned early through the tragic death of Nadab and Abihu that the holy fire was not to be imitated nor replaced (Leviticus 10:1-7). This is an old lesson, but one all those who share the Christian ministry, and all who aspire thereto, would do well to ponder.

"Strange fire" is the Bible term. How well it describes the carnal exhibition of counterfeit eloquence, insipid oratory, that the naive often receive as angelic, fake mountain-moving faith, and simulated, loveless martyrdom. Paul affirms they profit nothing. All this may appear to be furiously burning fire, when in reality it is only artificial excitement. Why accept strange fire when the genuine Pentecostal fire is yet burning and is available to every consecrated candidate?

Baptism of Fire

In chapter two we dealt at length with the message of John the Baptist and pointed out that the climax of his ministry was the part he played in officially

introducing Jesus as the Christ to his generation. To
those who wondered whether John might himself be
the Messiah he explained that he was a mere voice
of one who indeed baptized with water, but one who
said there is coming a greater Baptizer. "He shall
baptize you with the Holy Ghost, and with fire" (Matthew 3:11).

There is a school of Bible interpreters which
places a hyper-emphasis on water baptism, almost to
the point of baptismal regeneration, but which de-
nies that the phrase "with fire" is part of the promise to believers. Unfortunately many earnest Christians have done this service to the cause of Christ by
falling victims of the same error. They assert that two
alternatives are here offered, viz., the baptism with
the Holy Ghost or the baptism of hell fire. We need
not hesitate to brand this as an erroneous interpretation. It certainly was not the mission of Jesus in
coming to earth to offer the world a choice between
a baptism with the Holy Ghost and baptism with hell
fire. Such an interpretation is wholly unworthy of Jesus, for in no sense was His a mission to baptize with
hell fire. It was not to condemn but to save. As we
have seen, the word *fire* is associated with some
loftier uses than that of punishing the wicked in hell.

"Fire" in this instance refers to a particular manifestation of God the Holy Ghost, and conforms perfectly with the revelations of God the consuming
fire of Old Testament fame. It sets forth the office

work of the Holy Ghost in a special way, revealing a definite aspect of His work, "as opposed to water, which purifies by washing away, fire purifies by consuming and refining" (see Malachi 3:2).—P. C. Nelson in *Bible Doctrines*.

"Isaiah was both purified and fired for service by the 'live coal' taken from the altar (Isaiah 6:7), and laid on his mouth. As fire coming into cold, black iron can make it red, then pink, then white and glistening; so the Holy Spirit in the heart of the believer can soften and melt him and warm his cold nature, illuminating and inspiring him, and can make him like John, 'a burning and shining light' (John 3:35). John shone because he was 'on fire,' and so were the hundred and twenty at and after Pentecost. What would Pentecost be without the fire of the Holy Spirit?"—P. C. Nelson.

"The fire of God's Spirit is not a wrathful energy, working pain and death, but a merciful omnipotence, bringing light, and joy, and peace. The Spirit which is fire is a Spirit which giveth life . . . Christ comes to kindle in men's souls a blaze of enthusiastic Divine love, such as the world never saw, and to set them aflame with fervent earnestness, which shall melt all the icy hardness of heart, and turn cold self-regard into self-forgetting consecration."—A. Maclaren.

"Here is the power that produces that inner fervor without which virtue is a name and religion is a yoke. Here is the contrast, not only to John's baptism, but to all worldly religion, to all formalism, and decent deadness of external propriety. Here is the consecration of enthusiasm—not lurid, sullen heat of ignorant fanaticism, but a living glow of an enkindled nature, which flames because kindled by the inextinguishable blaze of His love who gave himself for us. 'He shall baptize you in fire.' "—A. Maclaren.

"Fire is the chosen symbol of heaven for moral passion. It is emotion aflame. God is love; God is fire. The two are one. The Holy Spirit baptizes in fire. Spirit-filled souls are ablaze for God. They love with a love that glows. They believe with a faith that kindles. They serve with a devotion that consumes. They hate sin with a fierceness that burns. They rejoice with a joy that radiates. Love is perfected in the fire of God."—Samuel Chadwick.

Commenting on the same passage Adam Clarke remarks: "He (the Spirit) is represented here under the similitude of fire, because he was to illuminate and purify the soul, penetrate every part and assimilate the whole to his own nature." This was the baptism John said he needed.

(For my comment on the fulfillment of the promised coming of the Holy Spirit see chapter four.)

Some Results of Pentecostal Fire

It is Pentecostal fire that prevails. Men ablaze with

this fire are invincible. The Pentecostal blessing came accompanied with "tongues like fire." But a real, holy, unearthly fire burned in the hearts of all who received the Holy Ghost baptism. It was the kind of fire Jeremiah said was shut up in his bones. Discouraged by a spiritless, backsliding people who disregarded his faithful warnings he had resolved to speak no more in His name. But he could not refrain, because, he asserted, "His word was in mine heart as a burning fire shut up in my bones" (Jeremiah 20:9). This fire was evidenced by the new attitude of the disciples. Their enthusiasm knew no bounds. They were seized by a new irrepressible drive that sent them into the world as sheep among wolves, like their Leader, as sheep to the slaughter.

It was Pentecostal fire that gave the church its voice. A church with such a Saviour must have such a voice. It cannot be dumb. With no pre-Pentecostal urge to bear witness for Christ they now "went forth and preached everywhere." Commanded to speak no more in His name, their answer was, "We cannot but speak," and their enemies complained, "You have filled Jerusalem with your doctrine." Later they were accused of turning the world upside down.

Their Great Commission was to bear witness to every creature unto the uttermost parts of the earth. Each generation takes it up with zeal to get the message to the last man. The fire continues to burn. Filled with the Spirit the church still pursues its course. It defies all barriers and challenges every foe. It sings its way and its faith through prisons, across continents and seas, over mountains and p l a i n s, through fires of persecution and through death, wherever men are found. It goes the second mile, gives away its cloak and turns the other cheek. It marches with the conqueror's tread because it is armed with the sword of the Spirit, the Word of God, and driven forward by a holy, burning obsession, the Holy Ghost and fire.

Lives Become Dynamic When Touched by Pentecostal Fire

Life can never remain the same when touched by Pentecostal fire. Moses, the refugee, shepherd-prince in seclusion in Midian saw the bush ablaze and as he beheld it he met the God of his fathers. During the forty full years of his remaining life the influence of that moment of destiny lived with him and was the impelling force that made him the great emancipator, law-giver and prophet of Israel. A flame was kindled that day in his heart that blazed until the day he fell asleep in the arms of God on Mt. Nebo.

Isaiah, the tender, princely prophet of Judah was content with the mediocre status quo until the day he saw the Lord high and lifted up. Then he saw the alarming but true picture of himself and his people, sinful and unclean. In a paroxysm of hearty contrition he mourned, "Woe is me." He lost sight of the magnificence of his surroundings in the Temple; he was no longer intrigued by the lavish ritual or the sweet melodies of the Levite choir. The prosperity their nation then enjoyed from the able administration of the late King Uzziah meant nothing now that he saw himself naked, vile, condemned and defenseless before God. "Woe is me" is the common lament of the sinner exposed to a view of the holiness of God in contrast with that of his own depraved self.

Notwithstanding the wide and guilty distance between the holiness of God and the sinfulness of man, the redeeming God has the panacea. It is the fire from the brazen altar—fire that burned at the place of, and because of the shed blood of Christ our Sacrifice (in this case in type only). The altar was the place of sacrifice for our objective justification. The fire from the altar to touch the life experimentally is the subjective counterpart of the vicarious transaction.

In love and grace the seraphim proceeded from the altar to the humbled, contrite prophet, with a live coal, placing it on his lips, and with the good news, "Lo, this hath touched thy lips; and thine iniquity is taken away, and thy sin purged." Immediately Isaiah was changed. Cleansed from all his sin and foulness he heard the voice of the Lord crying, "Who will go for us?" His was the response of a happy, holy heart, fired with new enthusiasm, "Here am I; send

me" (Isaiah 6). A mighty transformation was wrought
by the fire of God.

Go back and compare the picture of the pre-
Pentecostal disciples with the remarkable perform-
ances of the same group after they received the Holy
Ghost and fire. A mightier transformation cannot be
found in the annals of mankind. They were dynamic.
The power, the fiery zeal, the constraining love of
Christ had been transferred to them. They were radiant, they were fearless, they glowed in the very
city of Jerusalem where only fifty days before they
had suffered humiliating defeat.

Pentecostal Fire Produced True Togetherness

Previous mention has been made of the carnal rivalry that was so patent among the disciples. It was so
prevalent that it showed itself in some very solemn
moments and must have embarrassed both themselves and the Master. But that too is the pre-Pentecostal picture. Let us view the Pentecostal scene.
Pentecostal fire effected a brotherly cohesion hitherto unknown. As if under the spell of some magic
magnet, for the first time all were drawn to a common center, the Lord Jesus Christ. Their hopes, their
aims, their objectives were one. Their sole purpose
was now the exaltation of Christ. Their objectives
were His. How may we account for so radical a
change? What could have ever uprooted those in-

veterate personal ambitions that so many carry to the grave?

Dr. E. Stanley Jones, on the subject of Pentecostal fire, says it "fused the Church together." By way of explanation he calls attention to the manner in which the blacksmith welds iron. The cold, dark metal is left in the fire until it is filled with fire, until it is white and sparkling with heat. He then places it on the anvil. It is while at this stage of heat the iron is malleable and may be easily "fused" together. This could not happen to cold, fireless iron. Neither can it happen to cold, self-centered, carnal hearts. The fire of the Spirit purifies the hearts of the consecrated, cures of selfish ambitions, self assertiveness, and enables one to see, love and appreciate others.

In support of his illustration of "Fusion," Dr. Jones adduces the following Scripture references (but not the comment):

1. On the Day of Pentecost, in order to speak to the congregation, the record states, "Peter, standing up with the eleven" (Acts 2:14). Peter was not a "free lancer," nor a "lone wolf." The Church of which he was representative was destined to become "The pillar and ground of the Truth." Its message was not his own. It was not a matter of his own private interpretation. He knew the keys of the Kingdom were not his personal property. He did not wish to appear to be operating a side exhibition apart from the oth-

ers. The new-born church was "together," and op-
erated like a baseball team. He stood up with the
eleven and they stood with him. There was unity in
their message and in their purpose.

Under the anointing of the Holy Ghost Peter stood
to deliver the message of the meeting, but it was not
his message, nor his personal opinion. It was the message of the Church, which the Church had been
commissioned to preach to all the world beginning
at Jerusalem. The Church of God had, and still has,
one message though it be voiced in a thousand ways,
by a thousand tongues and extend from the days of
Peter until the Lord returns to earth. Anointed with
the Spirit one would preach no other. There need
be no fear that the Pentecostal fire will breed schism.
On the contrary it "fuses" hearts together. Schism
emanates from cold hearts that lose the vision of
Christ and others. Let those who become self-
enamored and lose sight of others and Christ, the
head of the Church, wait in humility before the
throne that is high and lifted up until they receive
the Pentecostal fire, and then behold a marvelous
transformation.

2. "Peter and John went up together into the temple at the hour of prayer" (Acts 3:1). This is a
worthy and most pertinent observation. It is noteworthy that it was "Peter and John." Why not Peter
and his brother Andrew? Or why not John and James?

Peter and John were unquestionably antagonists and the two "runners-up" in bidding for first place in the kingdom just forty days before. There has been a radical change in these two men, which calls for an explanation. But we need not look far for the answer. Both are now filled with the Holy Ghost. The feud is over, and it has left no rancorous feeling of rivalry. Whatever else the record may have omitted, it is clear on this point, "Peter and John were together." The Pentecostal fire has "fused" them together. The fire of God will certainly "fuse" the hearts of men into Christian unity if they will expose themselves to it.

Let God's people never fear the fire! But may it ever be the fire of God!

The priests in the Mosaic economy carried on their work in the light of the altar fires. There was no other light. In the holy place there were no windows, and consequently no other light than that from the golden candlestick, itself lighted by fire from the altar. Thus it was supernatural light. The fire of God must never go out because only in that light may the servants of God carry on His work.

Intellectualism, science, worldly erudition have their places in our modern world, but none of these can substitute for the baptism of fire promised and given to the Church of God on its inaugural day. Like jangled bells conflicting voices in the name of science and religion confuse the eternity destined traveler. There should be an infallible light. And there is.

Wherever the Pentecostal fire burns the light is aglow. Judaism could not put out its flame by orders, threats, persecution, or even murder. Skeptical Greek culture was no match for it. The indifference of the pagan world could not stifle it. It will burn until Christ gathers together all things in Himself. It should be aflame on the altar of every heart. It flames spontaneously when the individual meets the conditions of God's word in consecration.

CHAPTER VIII

PENTECOSTAL WITNESSING

Pentecostal Emphasis

SOME would have us believe that with the passing of the Day of Pentecost, which was a day of the extraordinary and abnormal, that there is now little necessity for emphasis on the Holy Spirit, and that simply to make the Christian confession is the *summum bonum.* That position, a decided departure from the Scripture, is the cause of great spiritual impoverishment. It is a tragic error, if not sacrelidgious, to attempt God's service in the energy of the flesh in lieu of the prescribed and promised power of the Holy Ghost. No one need do so, for the promise is still in vogue today.

Among the first Christians the Pentecostal experience became the official hallmark of qualification for Christian service. Since it was expected that every believer should be a witness for the Lord, it was also expected that all witnesses be Spirit-filled. Many cases have been lost at court because of a poor witness. The danger today is that our witnessing may fail because it is cold, professional, inane, mechanical and powerless. In those days men were recognized for positions of trust, not primarily because of special skill, but because they were "full of the Holy Ghost." The care taken in the selection of the first deacons is an example (Acts 6).

It was the miraculous outpouring of the Holy Ghost upon the Gentiles that convinced the Jewish brethren that God had opened the door of the Kingdom to them. Nothing short of a duplication of the results of the Day of Pentecost would have broken down their deep-rooted doubt and prejudice. The unprecedented action of Peter's going to minister to the Gentile house of Cornelius posed a real problem for the all-Jewish Apostolate who had restricted their ministry to their own nation. Peter found himself under the searching spotlight of scrutiny for committing what appeared to some to have been a breach of trust of the gospel committed to them. But his defense was wise. After giving a summary of the details of his being directed of the Spirit to accept the call of Cornelius and to go to his home doubting nothing, he continued, "As I began to speak, the Holy Ghost fell on them, as on us at the beginning. Then remembered I the word of the Lord . . . Ye shall be baptized with the Holy Ghost. Forasmuch then as God gave them the like gift as he did unto us, who believed on the Lord Jesus Christ; what was I, that I could withstand God?" (Acts 11:1-18).

His defense was overwhelmingly triumphant. The Apostles were thoroughly convinced and "glorified God, saying, Then hath God also to the Gentiles granted repentance unto life." The fact that they had received the Holy Ghost was sufficient proof to the most prejudiced of them, for "God bare them witness, giving them the Holy Ghost, even as he did unto us" (Acts 15:8).

The purpose of the references to the incidents of the selection of the first diaconate and of the Gentiles receiving the Holy Ghost is simply to point out the emphasis that the Church in the beginning placed on the Pentecostal experience. All were to bear witness, and all needed the same enduement of power. Nothing short of the repetition of the coming of the Holy Spirit as He had come to them on the Day of Pentecost ever would have convinced the prejudiced Jews that God had opened the way to Gentiles.

Pentecost and Evangelism

Evangelism has since the Day of Pentecost been the theme of the Spirit-filled. The wisdom of the ten days of waiting was justified in the light of the events that were set in motion on that day. They were indeed the "Ten days that changed the world." The Master had emphasized the importance of the advent of the Holy Ghost by ordering that everything stop and that no business, even in His name, be executed until the waiting disciples be "endued" with the power of the Holy Ghost. Then He said, "Ye shall be witnesses unto me . . . unto the uttermost part of the earth." It is the principle mission of the Comforter to "testify of me," said He, "And ye also shall bear witness."

The new-born Church lost no time in initiating the witnessing crusade. When the Holy Ghost came they straightway and openly began to publish the good news of salvation which was through the crucified, risen Saviour. They began at the very first meeting on the day the Comforter came. It was about nine o'clock in the morning when Peter stood up to deliver the first evangelistic message of the Church. The multitudes present in Jerusalem for the Feast of Pentecost from all over the known world wherever the Jews had b e e n scattered miraculously heard the gospel in their own languages. The devout acclaimed it the "Wonderful works of God." The climax of the meeting was the gospel invitation and the conversion of about three thousand.

This was the beginning of Christian world missions. The witnessing continued daily in the Temple, the market places, and from house to house. The witnesses, beginning in Jerusalem where they had suffered shameful frustration, were at once on their way to the uttermost parts of the earth. And it was crystal clear to all who knew the facts that the impelling urge to preach the gospel everywhere, though uninvited and often to the hostile and belligerent at the expense of life itself, was the direct result of the personal enduement of power which came upon them at Pentecost. "And with great power gave the apostles witness of the resurrection of the Lord Jesus: and great grace was upon them all" (Acts 4:33).

There are those who feel that witnessing is only the responsibility of the professional clergy. They excuse their own spiritual barrenness, supineness and lack of zeal on the pretext that they are only laymen. But they have overlooked a very important part of the record and have failed to receive the power the first Christians received for all—apostles and laymen alike—were mightily moved as "His witnesses" to "speak forth the things" they had "seen and heard." They were witnesses with a passion. Consider the following:

"And at that time there was a great persecution against the church which was at Jerusalem; and they were all scattered abroad throughout the regions of Judaea and Samaria, except the apostles." They were laymen. Notice, the Apostles remained in Jerusalem. Now what do you suppose happened to these victims of the dispersion? Did the fact that they were banished discourage, stifle or silence them? Did it quench the Pentecostal fire that had burned so brightly? Did they hold their peace because they were mere laymen? The answer is a matter of record: "Therefore they that were scattered abroad went every where preaching the word" (Acts 8:1-4). This is a grand testimonial of the zeal of laymen. They were participants of the same great power which came upon the Apostles. There is little in the New Testament that would lead one to think God is a respecter of persons or that he reserved special blessings for the Apostles which He did not wish to be shared by every Christian. It is unbelief that excuses spiritual poverty on the ground that it was only for Apostles or for the first Christians.

The Qualified Witness

A witness must have something to tell. It must be something he has seen, touched, heard, or personally experienced. A true witness must do more than repeat in parrot fashion something he has read or heard about Jesus Christ. He must possess some personal, first-hand knowledge of Him, which is corroborated by the Scriptures. A true witness of Jesus Christ must be able out of his own experience to verify the fact of a living Saviour. This is only possible through the ministry of the Holy Spirit. He must have experienced a personal revelation of Him. The convincing proof that so thoroughly satisfied the disciples who saw Him ascend heavenward on clouds of glory was the fulfillment of His own minutely explained, and oft-repeated promise to send another Comforter. "I will pray the Father, and he shall give you another Comforter." "I will not leave you comfortless: I will come to you." "At that day ye shall know that I am in my Father." "I . . . will manifest myself to him." "We will come unto him, and make our abode with him" (John 14). If any phase of the promise had failed, the disciples might have had every right to believe that Jesus had disappeared into everlasting oblivion. But it did not fail. They knew He was with the Father because the promised Comforter came to them. The coming of the Comforter into any life today is a fresh reminder of the fact that Jesus still reigns at the right hand of the Majesty in glory.

The reality and assurance of the living but invisible Christ is vividly represented by the tinkling bells on the garment of Israel's high priest as he ministered before the Lord in the holiest place in the tabernacle.

In that awesome moment while the high priest appeared in the august presence of God the penitent congregation stood without with fear and trembling, contritely confessing their sins, praying for mercy and waiting in suspense. They understood that they were accepted only in the person of the high priest. If he were accepted as he ministered before the mercy seat, the congregation was also accepted and their sins forgiven. Mindful of their sinfulness and their utter unworthiness of the favor they sought, they feared their representative might not survive the holy presence. Two of their priests had perished for their presumption while administering the priest's office, and rejection of the high priest meant rejection of the people. It was truly a soul-searching ordeal for sinful, mortal man to come into the presence of the holy and righteous God.

But in order to alleviate the fears of the waiting people God improvised a plan. The border of the high priest's garment was, according to the pattern given Moses, to be adorned with, in addition to other ornaments, golden bells. While he moved about in the performance of his sacred duties in the solitary place those on the other side of the veil could hear the sweet music of the tinkling bells. To them the sound was sweet and significant! The message of the bells was, "He lives, he lives." Their high priest was alive, and their sacrifice was accepted. They were justified. How eagerly those nearest the veil listened for their soft tones, and how joyfully they passed the word along, bearing witness until the last man in the congregation knew that the bells were ringing and all was well.

The sound of the tinkling bells from the inner sanctum, like a still small voice, was a revelation. The gentle cadence so laden with hope was a prophecy of the day ordained of God when Christ our great high priest should enter the Holy of Holies in the true tabernacle which the Lord pitched in heaven. There He would appear in the presence of God for us. It also signified the assuring revelation He would shed forth in the person of the Holy Ghost. All who would receive that precious promise of the Father would know that Jesus was "in the Father" alive for evermore. The testimony of the Spirit is the antitype of the bells. It is the presence of the Spirit in the individual heart that sets the joy bells ringing, and assures the believer that our great High Priest lives. Faithful to the word of Jesus, the Comforter testifies of Him, that "He lives, He lives."

It should be noted that there were present in ancient Israel as well as in our day two kinds of witnesses: those who could testify to the facts of the living high priest because they had heard the bells, and those who could only say that had heard one who heard another say he had heard the bells. Only he who has heard for himself is a qualified witness. Those baptized with the Holy Ghost are qualified.

This writer concedes according to the Scripture that there are many who are born of the Spirit (John 3:3-8), who "have the Spirit" (Romans 8:9), but who are not "filled with the Spirit" nor "baptized with the Spirit." However it seems fitting to make this observation: the Scriptures are written for high level Christian living. They make no allowance for sub-Pentecostal experience after the day of Pentecost came. It is the scriptural position that all believers should avail themselves of the full benefits of the Holy Spirit. It was expected, according to the Early Church Fathers that all converts should receive the baptism of the Holy Ghost and speak with tongues. Granting that

there are many who have not arrived at this high
spiritual level, the minister of the Word of God must
remain faithful to the Word. He dare not reduce the
standard because so few come up to it. He dare not
come down to the popular level.

Enough has been said to convince any unbiased in-
vestigator that in the primitive church it was the rule
that every witness must have been baptized with the
Holy Ghost. This was not an iron-fisted rule designed
to proscribe anyone from ministerial liberty, because
the promise was to all, "as many as the Lord our God
shall call." To ignore or to reject the proffered enduement of power was little less than an affront to
the Divine Giver. No one had a right to preach the
gospel without the enduement, and no one then or
now need do so. The blessing is available to "them
that obey him" (Acts 5:32). No other qualification
can substitute for that required by the Lord Himself:
Receive ye the Holy Ghost.

The First Foreign Missionaries

The story of the first Christian missionary project
is a unique revelation of the ministry of the Spirit.
One cannot read it without being impressed with the
utter dependence of the Church upon the Holy Spirit.
It seems never to have occurred to them to rely upon
mere "showmanship," or to make a display of human talents or wisdom. Only the Holy Ghost could

"convict" of sin and cause men to cry out, "Men and brethren, what shall we do to be saved?"

The Scripture record of the selection, sending forth and reliance of the first missionaries upon the Holy Ghost is most provocative. The Holy Ghost was present at every juncture to direct and to help their infirmities. See the record:

"As they ministered to the Lord, and fasted, the Holy Ghost said, Separate me Barnabas and Saul for the work whereunto I have called them. And when they had fasted and prayed, and laid their hands on them, they sent them away. So they, being sent forth by the Holy Ghost, departed" (Acts 13:1-4).

When withstood by Satan at Paphos through sorcerer Barjesus, "Then Saul, (who also is called Paul,) filled with the Holy Ghost, set his eyes on him, And said, . . . thou shalt be blind, not seeing the sun for a season. And immediately there fell on him a mist and a darkness; and he went about seeking some to lead him by the hand" (Acts 13:8-11).

When their converts in Antioch in Pisidia suffered the shock of great opposition and saw the Apostles driven from their midst, the Holy Ghost saved them from despair. "And the disciples were filled with joy, and with the Holy Ghost" (Acts 13:52).

Confronted with the vexing problem of legalism which compelled the missionaries to appeal to the Jerusalem Council, the group handed down the decree which contained the powerful words: "It seemed good to the Holy Ghost, and to us" (Acts 15:28). How truly the great Paraclete directed in subduing the schism that would have torn the church asunder! His presence gave authority to their deliberations and enabled them to arrive at a wise and peaceful solution of a tremendous problem.

On the second missionary journey the path of Paul and Silas was chosen by the Holy Ghost. When they would erroneously have ventured into Asia they "were forbidden of the Holy Ghost" (Acts 16:6). "They assayed to go into Bithynia: but the Spirit suffered them not" (Acts 16:7). After a vision of a man of Macedonia praying, "Come over . . . and help us" they set out toward Europe, "Assuredly gathering that the Lord had called" them "to preach the gospel unto them" (Acts 16:9, 10).

With reference to these marvelous directions of the Spirit it is noteworthy that upon their arrival at the appointed fields of labor that the Holy Ghost there confirmed the preaching of the Word and set his approval upon the laborers and their work. This provides us with a worthy precedent. Those who profess to be directed by the Spirit should be able to point to a Spirit-approved ministry.

To the end, this missionary program was from the Holy Ghost. The wisdom of following the Spirit is vindicated in the marvelous manner in which the gospel subsequently was preached in the lands where the missionaries were forbidden to go. The record of the Acts of the Apostles is ample explanation. It is a challenge to all who would know of God's method of carrying on God's business.

All that has been said about Pentecostal witnessing may be summed up in one brief sentence: Pentecost produces a passion for souls. It has been well stated by a great missionary that there is "No sterner test of Pentecost than the attitude toward the lost." "The first test of Pentecost was, how much do you love Jesus? The second test was, how much do you value man?"—L. R. Scarborough, D.D., LL.D. Certainly there is no more accurate test. The Spirit-filled are always solicitous and tender toward the lost. Beholding men without Christ through tears of holy compassion, they "Go forth weeping, bearing precious seed." Thus it was that the glorious and sweeping awakening immediately followed Pentecost. How vividly this is exemplified by the Apostle Paul in Romans 8, where he has expounded at length on the work of the Holy Spirit. Nineteen times in that chapter he has referred to the Spirit. But that is not the end. His burning compassion bursts right into the next chapter where it reaches a grand climactic crescendo in the following heartbreaking expression: "I say the truth in Christ, I lie not, my conscience also bearing me witness in the Holy Ghost, That I have great heaviness and continual sorrow in my heart. For I could wish that myself were accursed from Christ

for my brethren, my kinsmen according to the flesh"
(Romans 9:1-5).

Let all who make claims of the Pentecostal experience tread softly in the presence of this self-abasing,
consuming, magnificent obsession. Wholly obsessed
with Christ and the "good news" more than sixty million Christians have become martyrs rather than give
up their testimony. The word *martyr* became the
synonym of "witness." To be a witness often meant
to be a martyr.

Confronted with witnesses whose souls were
aflame with this holy fervor the Jerusalem mob so recently guilty of crucifying the Saviour was "pricked in
their hearts" and melted to repentance. Before the
apostle with burning heart, the dissolute Felix with
a heart of stone lost his composure and "trembled."

Witnesses must be filled with the Spirit for only
"He will convict the world of sin."

CHAPTER IX

THE PENTECOSTAL ANOINTING

ANOINTING occupied a prominent place in the exercise of Old Testament religious ceremony. The expression "anoint" or its equivalent appears in some form at least one hundred fifty times in the Bible. It is said to be found in twenty-two books of the Old Testament and in ten of the New Testament. Both persons and inanimate objects were anointed as acts of consecration. Prophets, priests and kings were anointed when they entered office. Anointing denoted setting apart or sealing for special service. It was an official act that marked a person or place for the service of God.

Anointing Oil

The rite of anointing was performed by pouring, smearing, or rubbing oil upon the person or thing to be consecrated. The kind of oil originally used for this purpose is not known, but in the time of Moses oil of olive berries was prescribed. Moses directed the compounding of a perfumed oil, which was known as "an oil of holy ointment" and "an holy anointing oil" (Exodus 30:22-25; Psalm 33).

The holy anointing oil was composed of myrrh, sweet cinnamon, sweet calamus, cassia and olive oil. This was a very special and sacred oil, as is indicated by the description "holy" and "precious," and also by the following prohibitions:

1. "Upon man's flesh shall it not be poured" (Exodus 30:32). It was not to be used for any secular or private purpose; its use was restricted to prophets, priests, kings and sacred objects.

2. It was not to be imitated nor substituted. "Whosoever compoundeth any like it . . . shall even be cut off from his people" (Exodus 30:33).

3. It was not to be put "upon a stranger."

The importance of the holy anointing is obvious because of the fact that, whatever the status of the individual, he was not qualified for service without the anointing. One might have been a member of the royal family and next in the line of succession to the throne, but he could not be king without the anointing. David was already a son of Israel, and of the royal tribe of Judah, but that did not make him king. Looking upon his heart God saw one after his own heart, but there remained the matter of anointing to qualify and distinguish him as God's choice.

David's brothers, all more mature and more prepossessing than the young shepherd, impressed Samuel more than David did. By his natural powers of deduction Samuel saw no particular virtue in him, and would have accepted any one of his brothers in preference to him, but David received the anointing, at which time "the Spirit of the Lord came upon him" (1 Samuel 16:1-13). It is apparent from this incident that the anointing makes a difference and is a mark of particular distinction.

Oil: A Symbol of the Holy Spirit

The anointing oil, prepared according to divine instructions was a fitting symbol of the Holy Spirit. Properly administered, it was a symbol of the endowment of the Spirit of God for the purpose of enablement for the performance of duties of the office to which the recipient was called and consecrated. Thus the anointing with the holy oil provided a graphic preview of the Pentecostal anointing of the Holy Spirit which in the "last days" was to become the distinctive mark of qualification upon those consecrated to the service of God. Whatever may be one's status in the family of God, it is thus that he is commissioned for the official function as an ambassador for Christ. It is by the anointing of the Spirit that the ambassador receives power for service—both authority (Greek, *exousian)* and ability (*dunamis)* (Matthew 28:18; Mark 6:7; Acts 1:8).

In support of this position no worthier example could be cited than that of our Lord Jesus Christ. Announcing His ministry in His home synagogue at Nazareth, He read from the prophet Isaiah (61:1): "The Spirit of the Lord is upon me, because he hath anointed me to preach the gospel to the poor" (Luke 4:18-21). When He had finished the reading he declared, "This day is this scripture fulfilled in your ears." This passage makes it clear that having the Spirit upon him and having the "anointing" were synonymous.

Referring to the anointing of Christ, the author of Hebrews quotes from Psalm 45:7, "Therefore God, even thy God, hath anointed thee with the oil of gladness above thy fellows" (Hebrews 1:9). The word *Christ* means, "The anointed one." The oil of gladness, it is quite clear, was the Spirit of the Lord. How marvelous that the coming of the Holy Spirit should have been so appropriately, beautifully and prophetically portrayed in the anointing with the precious, fragrant, holy anointing oil!

The two preceding passages (Luke 4:18 and Hebrews 1:9) speak of two events in the career of Jesus. First, He was anointed with the Holy Ghost at the time of His baptism by John in the River Jordan (Matthew 3:16). The second reference concerns something that happened to Jesus after He had passed through His probation and proved that He "loved righteousness, and hated iniquity (Hebrews 1:9).

This anointing took place on the Day of Pentecost while Jesus was at the right hand of the heavenly Father. "Therefore being by the right hand of God exalted, and having received of the Father the promise of the Holy Ghost, he hath shed forth this, which ye now see and hear" (Acts 2:33). This was Peter's explanation of what was happening in the first Pentecostal meeting. It was the fulfillment of the Father's promise to Jesus as head of the body, the Church. This fact is prophetically illustrated in Psalm 133: "It is like the precious ointment . . . that ran down upon the beard, even Aaron's beard: that went down to the skirts of his garments." The anointing of Aaron as high priest, inasmuch as the high priest of Israel stood for all of Israel, represented the acceptance and anointing of the entire nation. When the holy anointing was poured forth upon Jesus, our great High Priest and Head of the Church, on the Day of Pentecost, it ran down upon every member of the body, all present at the meeting. It runs down to our present generation and is for the greatest or for the least and most remote member of the Church, or for every convert to the end of the age.

By way of clarification it should be observed, with respect to those who claim that this was the baptism of the Holy Ghost for the entire church age once and for all, that only those present at that meeting received the blessing, and that those who believed on the Lord at future dates also received similar personal experiences. Long after the Day of Pentecost the Apostles were still preaching and speaking of the anointing, proving that it did not end with the occurrence of Pentecost. To the Corinthians Paul wrote that, "Now he which stablisheth us with you in Christ, and hath anointed us, is God" (2 Corinthians 1:21).

The beloved Apostle John as late as A.D. 90 rejoiced with his people that "Ye have an unction from the Holy One, and ye know all things . . . But the anointing which ye have received of him abideth in you, and ye need not that any man teach you: but as the same anointing teacheth you of all things" (1 John 2:20, 27). (The word *unction* means "anointing.") Lest someone misunderstand the ministry of the Spirit in this case, John's reference to teaching was not to the sciences, history, the fine arts or literature, but to a supersensory enablement to discern the times, the activities of the Antichrist spirit and Christian duty in following the truth. This is his function today.

It also appears that John would make a distinction between the anointed and the unanointed. Some, he says, had gone out from them, erring, straying from the truth, because "they are not of us." But it was not the anointed for they who retained the anointing knew the truth. The anointing made a visible difference in John's day.

What a thrilling blessing it is to know that everyone may share in the anointing. It was no special dispensation of grace limited to apostolic times, but it is still on the authorized agenda and is available to every member of the body of Christ "as many as the Lord our God shall call."

Some Effects of the Anointing

There are many blessed products of the Pentecostal anointing, some of which have been discussed in previous chapters. However here are two of great magnitude worthy of special mention.

1. The Pentecostal anointing is the seal of God upon His people. This statement is made advisedly and not unmindful of the many fine friends who may disagree with it. The pertinent passage that states "Having this seal, The Lord knoweth them that are his" (2 Timothy 2:19) has not been overlooked. This writer would not disparage nor deny the inner witness of the Spirit to the sonship of the believer. However he would remind the reader again that the New Testament was written to people who had a fresh recollection of Pentecost and at a time when it was expected that all believers should receive the Pentecostal anointing. With this thought in mind let us notice Ephesians 1:13: "You also have heard the message of truth, the gospel of your salvation, and in him you also by your faith have been stamped with the seal of the long-promised Holy Spirit."—Moffatt. It would be difficult to dissociate the "long-

promised Holy Spirit" or "the Holy Spirit of Promise,"
according to Authorized Version from the "promise
of the Father" of Luke 24:49. It is cheerfully ad-
mitted that the Lord has many blessed saints who
have not known and may never know the joy of the
Pentecostal anointing, and that the Lord knows them
every one. This is not a question of anyone's personal
salvation. Nevertheless, it is singularly true that while
the Lord knows all His own, the enemy knows those
who live with the anointing of the Spirit upon them.
The seal of anointing is the special mark of identity
and of authority of those who are set forth and "made
a spectacle unto the world, and to angels, and to
men" (1 Corinthians 4:9). Evil spirits know those
who bear the Pentecostal anointing. It certainly was
not without foreseeing the future and evaluating the
opposition that Jesus required that His disciples be
"endued with power" before attempting to convert a
hostile world.

2. The Pentecostal anointing will break every fetter
that binds the servant of God. The following promise concerning the anointing is a priceless gem:

"And it shall come to pass in that day, that his
burden shall be taken away from off thy shoulder,
and his yoke from off thy neck, and the yoke shall
be destroyed because of the anointing" (Isaiah
10:27).

The prophecy concerns, first, the yoke of bondage

of the Assyrians over the house of David. The last clause of the verse is literally translated, "The yoke shall be destroyed from before the oil." The meaning as it was then understood, was simply that the bondage would be terminated because on the house of David was the holy anointing oil.

It is the anointing that liberates men to preach the word (Isaiah 61:1). How men who know its meaning pray for the anointing that they may labor effectively! It was the anointing that broke the fetters of the defeated disciples when they were hiding with fear and trembling. It was the anointing that sent them forth joyously proclaiming the good news. Is there less need of anointed men and women in this atomic age than in any previous age? The unutterable cry of the needy world, as well as of an anemic, starving church, is: "Wanted: anointed leaders."

Anointing and Healing

It is the holy anointing that heals the sick. We are taught to pray for the sick, "Anointing him with oil in the name of the Lord" (James 5:14). Surely the anointing with simple olive oil is no panacea for all manner of sickness. It was not intended as a medicine. The oil is only a symbol of the Spirit, which the sick may expect to come upon them as Spirit-filled elders of the church lay hands upon them, anointing, and praying for them. The sick should be taught to expect a manifestation of the Spirit simultaneous with the anointing of oil. It is the Spirit's anointing which produces healing. The promise in connection with anointing and prayer is that "The Lord shall raise him up."

Anointing the sick—unction, as it was called—became a sacrament of the Catholic Church. St. Augustine, St. Bede and others believed and practiced it. Many of their ancient authorities insisted that it was to "save from death and keep alive." Gradually unspiritual leaders began to regard the "holy oil" as the "church's medicine," and to claim that the "effect on the body is not something of a miraculous order: the sacrament operates as a remedy." "Since the twelfth century, it has been the custom to describe the anointing of the sick as 'Extreme unction,' and the sacrament of the dying."—*Death and the Christian* by Jean Charles Didier. Later he adds, "Thus giving it that alarming meaning it now has."

But thanks be to our never changing Saviour, the Lord still heals the sick in confirmation of His own word and that of the Apostle James. There are many who still believe the Word, and anoint the sick, and the Lord still raises them up.

The Pentecostal anointing is indeed a blessed and a precious experience. It is the anointing of the Spirit that gives Christians liberty. It makes one conscious of the liberty we have in Christ, a freedom that prison walls cannot violate; it gives joy in tribulation, inspires songs in the night, gives hope in the dungeon; it makes one a spendthrift in the unsearchable riches of Christ, though he be otherwise penniless. It is the anointing indeed that breaks the yoke.

The anointing of Aaron has already been suggested as prophetically illustrating the Pentecostal anointing and its correlated results and implications. Yet so simple is the illustration, and its message so elusive that its gravity to the cursory reader may be entirely missed. Let us take a last view at Psalm 133, where the anointing of Aaron is described and compared to the blessedness of the unity of brethren.

When Moses anointed Aaron to be high priest of Israel, a copious profusion of the perfumed oil ran down from his head to his beard, to his garments and to the floor, while sweet aroma permeated and pervaded the atmosphere. On the fragile wings of the delightful fragrance was carried a silent message of good news—news that Israel now had an acceptable mediator. The anointing was proof of his acceptance. The silent aroma clinging to his garments announced to all that he was the anointed. In like manner, about the anointed is an aura of heavenly love, tense with the inimitable radiance of the Holy Spirit. His presence is overwhelmingly effective. Like the delicate mists of sweet odors, silent, unobtrusive, inoffensive, and charming, the unseen Spirit is eloquently persuasive. The Holy Spirit's influence, always a rebuke to sin, is able to insinuate itself discreetly into the service of divine worship, into our prayers, our hymns and sermons. It is He who arrests the attention and produces conviction. No one remains passive in the presence of the Pentecostal anointing. It alerts the imagination, breaks down honest objections and disarms resistance. It draws the earnest inquirer from indifference and distraction and exposes him to the truth. Just as beautiful perfume succeeds in making us forget unpleasant odors, His presence supplants unfavorable impressions and prejudices and awakens the conscience to the wooings of Christ.

Thus does the Pentecostal anointing grace the house of worship and the place of prayer. It is in this manner that the Holy Spirit "convicts the world of sin, of righteousness and of judgment." Thus does he glorify Christ. He is working while men sleep and while the laborers are weary and at the end of their wits with the burdens of the cause, and while results are not apparent.

Let us ever covet earnestly a rich, up-to-date anointing of the Spirit. And may we be assured that the Holy Spirit is fulfilling his function of making our message of truth effective in the hearts of those who hear.

CHAPTER X

PENTECOST AND PRAYER

PRAYER—a common word among people of all religions—is not so easy to define. Even in Christianity it does not yield to a simple, general definition. It has as many facets as a diamond, and one aspect in common acceptance among one branch of religion may be wholly unknown to another. In practice prayer ranges from quiet meditation to mechanical manipulations, such as the turning of a prayer wheel, the use of the rosary, the beating of drums, lacerating the body, burning incense, and shouted jaculations. Prayers are read from prayer books, chanted, recited eloquently, uttered informally and shouted passionately and extemporaneously. They consist of supplications, intercessions, thanksgiving, imprecations, and praise. If we understand prayer to be man's attempt to commune with his God it is the most primitive of religious exercises.

Since his expulsion from the Garden of Eden man has demonstrated himself to be instinctly a religious creature. He has built altars, shrines and temples where, amid joys and calamities, he has sought communion with God—often a God he did not know. His rites of religion have varied vastly, but they reveal that inherently man, though depraved and rebellious, is obsessed with a desire to be in communion with his god—not necessarily the true God—but his god.

Since the call of Abraham and God's revelation to him, prayer in the sense of communion with the Creator has been the very soul of worship. God, among the Israelites, was thought of as "The God that heareth prayer." While Israel endeavored to keep covenant with Him, prayer was purposeful, highly intelligent and proved to be the pivot on which many momentous events of their history turned from defeat to triumph. However, their prayer victories do not appear to have been the common lot of the average citizen of Israel, for prior to the Day of Pentecost Israel was represented before God by her priests and prophets. They were expected to know God, and some of them enjoyed gracious fillings of the Spirit, but such experiences were rare, extraordinary exceptions.

As has been explained in chapter six, Pentecost produced a sweeping revolution and ushered in a new order which gave everyone the right to be filled with the Spirit. The Spirit would recognize no barriers of separation between the priesthood and laymen, male or female, master or servant. Obviously when all the people of the New Testament church were filled with the Holy Ghost, their prayer gained tremendous momentum. Prayer along with the Word of God became the church's most powerful weapon of offense. The Apostles stressed, "Prayer, and to the ministry of the word" (Acts 6:4).

This was according to the Master's prediction. In the long discourse in which He explained with considerable detail the functions of the coming Comforter to the disciples as He walked with them en route to Gethsemane immediately after the Last Supper, He spoke of the new era which would dawn with His coming as "that day." Three times that same night He employed the term, "that day" (John 14:20; 16:23, 26). His reference to it without designating a particular date was so casual as to lead one to believe it had been discussed frequently enough that all understood it to refer to the period of time beginning with the advent of the Holy Ghost. The following verses show that the new era offered something decidedly new with reference to prayer: "And in that day ye shall ask me nothing. Verily, verily, I say unto you, Whatsoever ye shall ask the Father in my name, he will give it you. Hitherto have ye asked nothing in my name: ask, and ye shall receive, that your joy may be full. . . . At that day ye shall ask in my name: and I say not unto you, that I will pray the Father for you" (John 16:23-26).

There had been instances of mighty praying in the

Old Testament, but they were to be multiplied in the new era because the Spirit was to be poured out upon "all flesh," and because the Holy Spirit within the believer would intercede through Him, and Christ at the right hand of the Father would endorse all petitions offered in His name. Praying in the Spirit would without a doubt be "in his name." On this we shall elaborate further, endeavoring to show the advantages provided by the Holy Spirit's assisting our prayers.

The New Testament contains many urgent exhortations to pray, but none more pithy and relevant than the following: "And take the helmet of salvation, and the sword of the Spirit, which is the word of God: Praying always with all prayer and supplication in the Spirit . . ." (Ephesians 6:17, 18). But ye, beloved, building up yourselves on your most holy faith, praying in the Holy Ghost" (Jude 20). The phrases, "prayer and supplication in the Spirit" and "praying in the Holy Ghost," are peculiar to the New Testament. The use of these terms indicate that the new era—"that day"—had arrived in fulfillment of the Old Testament prophecy and the prediction of Christ. Let us examine the prophecy of Zechariah 12:10 on this subject, written about 487 B.C.: "And I will pour upon the house of David, and upon the inhabitants of Jerusalem, the spirit of grace and of supplications." This passage is parallel and similar to the one quoted by Peter at Pentecost, "This is that spoken by the prophet Joel, It shall come to pass afterward, that I will pour out my spirit upon all flesh" (Joel 2:28-32). Both passages received partial fulfillment at Pentecost for both referred to the event of the Advent of the Holy Ghost. Peter could have quoted this one also and said, "This is that spoken by the prophet Zechariah."

A simple analysis of the precious promise of the Father through the prophecy of Zechariah will result in the discovery of a mine of spiritual wealth which belongs to every Spirit-filled believer. Consider its principal parts:

1. *"Will pour out."* This is the same expression employed by Joel with reference to the new wine—the symbol of the Holy Spirit—which God would pour out in profusion on "that day." The record in Acts shows that he did so, and that "They were all filled with the Holy Ghost" (Acts 2:4). "The Holy Ghost; Which he shed on us abundantly" (Titus 3:5, 6).

2. *"The Spirit of Grace."* Grace simply means favor. The coming of the Holy Spirit into any life gives the recipient special rights and favors in the presence of God. It elevates him to the position of sonship. It is his assurance of "access" to the Father's throne. "For through him we both (Jews and Gentiles) have access by one Spirit unto the Father" (Ephesians 2:18).

It is marvelous grace which permits a mortal man upon whom the Spirit has been poured according to the promise to enter the Holy of Holies at his own discretion and have audience with the Father. There are those who appear to be especially gifted in prayer, to whom many go with multitudinous requests because it is felt that they can readily reach the ear and heart of God. With no thought of disparaging anyone so honored, let every believer be filled with the Spirit and accept his rightful inheritance to "Come boldly unto the throne of grace" (Hebrews 4:16). What favor! Along with the promise of the Father has come the Spirit of grace.

This is the answer to Satan's eternal reproaching by which he intimidates the Christian and deters him from the place of prayer. He finds it quite simple to convince us of our unworthiness, and he never ceases to harass us on that basis. About all we can do is to confess that we deserve nothing, for one never feels smaller or more helpless than when he humbly bows in the presence of the eternal God. But the coming of the Holy Spirit—and also the discovery of our rights according to the Word of God through the Spirit—is the answer to our need and a sufficient rejoiner with which to silence the adversary. The truth is, He has given us the Spirit of grace," and grace is only needed when we do not qualify on the basis of merit. One need make no false claims. Let him acknowledge his demerit, his unworthiness, but also let him boldly claim his rights as a son in the great Father's family, and take his place at "the throne of grace." The abiding Spirit will give him access. This is a most assuring privilege. Grasp it and go often to the Holy of Holies and commune with the heavenly Father.

3. *"The Spirit of Supplication."* This is the Spirit of Prayer. Thus it is evident that the Holy Spirit comes to us for very practical reasons. Praying is a big job and as we shall see further in this discussion, it is one that requires not only our best, but also the support of the Holy Spirit. Someone has remarked that it does not take much of a man to be a Christian, but it takes all there is of him. It takes more than our best, and God has provided us His best, the Comforter.

It is literally amazing how many events, great and small, occur in this world because someone prayed. For example, Peter was released from prison while the church was at prayer. Also, the seeming chance that kept sleep from the eyes of King Ahasuerus and which led to his reading the record of Mordecai's unrewarded service, and to the salvation of the Jews, all because the Jews fasted and prayed. Do not underestimate its importance. So imperative is it that God has provided power from on high to enable his people to pray effectively.

The Spirit of supplication is that power. It is "the

Spirit of his Son . . . in the heart of Christians . . . crying, Abba, Father" (Galatians 4:6). He prompts the believer to pray, and that often at very unexpected times under most amazing circumstances. He assists our prayers. He fills us with a desire to pray, gives words, often inspires one to tears and groans that cannot be uttered. He removes the aversion and disinclination to pray by bringing us into a frame of mind that makes prayer possible and delightful.

The Holy Spirit meets a very definite personal need in this direction of which every Christian is aware. Notice how aptly the Apostle states it: "And in like manner the Spirit also helpeth our infirmity: for we know now how to pray as we ought, but the Spirit, himself, maketh intercession for us with groanings which cannot be uttered" (Romans 8:26, 27 A.V.).

How often God's people are alerted to prayer at the bidding of the Spirit, to intercede for those in peril, for those passing through great and fiery trials, or for the lost. Granted that we are too feeble to carry our own burdens, much less those of others and that we know not how we ought to pray, the Holy Spirit is never at a loss for ways and means to accomplish His purposes. He resorts to supernatural means. It is not uncommon for those who have made prayer their ministry and who have consistently waited on their ministry to experience seasons of copious weeping before the Lord. Like Jeremiah, their eyes literally become fountains of tears. There are times when the inexpressible anguish of the soul can only vent itself with unutterable groanings. But let none despise this humbling before God. It is soul travail, and is prompted by the Holy Spirit. Let it suffice to know that "He that searcheth the hearts knoweth what is the mind of the Spirit" (Romans 8:27). Do not disparage, nor discount the tears that flow as mere signs of weakness when offered before God in intercessions. God does not consider them as signs of weakness, but has them in His bottle (Psalm 56:8). His blessing is upon "him that goeth forth weeping bearing precious seed." There will be a curtain call for him. "He shall doubtless come again with rejoicing, bringing his sheaves with him" (Psalm 126:6).

Earnest prayer "in the Holy Ghost" may also frequently be in a supernatural language.[1] There are special instances when the Holy Spirit lifts the sup-

---

1. There may be those who will object that there is in this discussion an over-emphasis on the baptism of the Holy Spirit on the pretext that every believer is a partaker of the Holy Ghost. We agree heartily that every Christian is born of the Spirit and has the Spirit abiding in him. The objector may feel that all that has been said is equally applicable to every Christian. But may we remind the reader that the New Testament standard is for maximum Christian living. Pentecost, with the baptism in the Holy Ghost for everyone, was God's ideal. While many a wonderful Christian may only know of a Pentecostless experience, it would appear folly to accept their position as the criterion in lieu of what is written in God's Word. It is not too late to receive the Holy Ghost baptism. Do not think of receiving this experience as a "penalty," but as a high and wonderful privilege. Do not be content with a minimum, subnormal experience.

plicant out of the sphere of the natural and sensuous
into the realm of the Spirit. When it is realized that
the Christian warfare is not physical nor intellectual, but a very real conflict with a very real spirit
world, we marvel at the wisdom of God in sending the Comforter to equip the believer for spiritual
warfare. "Let not the mighty man glory in his might";
it is no match for the powers of darkness. Intellectualism and sophistication without the Spirit are powerless in spiritual warfare. They can never deliver the
bound from chains of sin and Satan. Our victory is
"Not by might, nor by power, but by my spirit, saith
the Lord of hosts" (Zechariah 4:6).

Therefore, under the sway of the Holy Spirit the
believer is often exercised in "Wrestling against prin-
cipalities, against powers, against the rulers of the
darkness of this world, against spiritual wickedness
in high places" (Ephesians 6:12). Notice the reading of the same passage in the Goodspeed translation: "For we have to struggle, not with the enemies of flesh and blood, but with the hierarchies, the
authorities, the master-spirits of this dark world, the
spirit-forces of evil on high." Therefore, "the weap-
ons of our warfare are not carnal, but mighty through
God to the pulling down of strong holds" (2 Corinthians 10:4). Thanks be unto God who has fore-
seen the need and provided full armour for the Christian soldier. This in a true sense involves "Praying in

the Holy Ghost" (Jude 20).[2] Such prevailing prayer brings results.

The most sincere Christians are not infrequently embarrassed because the satanic opposition abases them with his old instrument of intimidation, particularly in having them doubt that their prayers are according to the will of God. But everyone can discern when he is praying in the Holy Ghost. Whether he understands all the implications or not, he will not fail to recognize the "lift" of the Spirit. Only those who have experienced it can appreciate the wonderful way He helps our infirmities. The discovery and grasping of this truth can be an invaluable blessing and a source of genuine comfort, because we will have learned to depend upon him who "maketh intercession for the saints according to the will of God" (Romans 8:27). Convinced that prayer is according to His will, doubt and intimidation disappear, and the petitioner has cause for rejoicing. He is assured since praying in the Holy Ghost that he has prayed according to the will of God and that his plea has reached the throne of our great High Priest.

As a matter of emphasis let it be reiterated that praying is a herculean undertaking. Those who are

---

2. With reference to praying in the Holy Ghost (Jude 20), "Praying in the Spirit" (I Cor. 14:14, 15), "Spiritual Songs" (Eph. 5:19, Col. 3:16), Rev. Carl Brumback in *What Meaneth This*, an excellent classic on Pentecost, is of the opinion that these expressions refer to the Glossalalia or speaking with other tongues. This writer concurs with that opinion, and recommends the reading of the book, which may be purchased at the Church of God Publishing House, Cleveland, Tennessee.

content with reading prayers or the dramatic recitation of rhetorical eloquence which can only satisfy their own vanity, or the utterance of meaningless prattle, have not understood the extreme gravity the New Testament accords the subject. To really appreciate its seriousness would certainly make one feel his need of the power of the Holy Spirit to make him efficient in prayer. Let us consider and evaluate the true character of prayer:

1. *Prayer is a form of labor.* "Epaphras, who is one of you, a servant of Christ, saluteth you, always labouring fervently for you in prayers" (Colossians 4:12). So few have thought of prayer in this light. Prayer is as definitely a part of the Christian's business as preaching, or ministering to the sick or needy. It should be as much a part of our life program as going to our daily business. Instead of being hurriedly crowded into our busy schedule wherever and whenever we can spare a moment, it should have priority, for prayer is the highest type of labor. When considered in this vein much so-called prayer is eliminated because it offers the Spirit so little opportunity to make supplications through us. If we would major in prayer the problems of life would be more easily mastered.

It has been said that the battle of Waterloo was won at Oxford University. That is not difficult to believe. An equally logical axiom is that our great battles are won at the place of prayer. It is quite evident then that to work well is to pray well, and vice versa.

This writer once saw a very interesting cartoon of a man cutting wood on a hot summer day with a dull ax. Beads of sweat poured copiously from his face and brow while he paused for a moment of rest. A wise and friendly neighbor advised him that if he would sweat more on the grind stone he would not have to sweat so much on the wood pile. May we learn from this the timely lesson that if God's people would give themselves more to laboring in prayer, their labors in the energy of the flesh would be reduced. If our greatest work is accomplished in and through prayer, is it not a mystery that God's people do not pray more?

2. *Prayer may be agonizing.* Said Paul, "Whereunto I also labour, striving according to his working, which worketh in me mightily" (Colossians 1:29). The Greek word translated striving is also translated "agonize." The translation could also have been, "I also labour agonizing." Only once does the word *agony* appear in the Bible, and it is in connection with the supreme example of prayer: "And being in an agony he prayed" (Luke 22:44). There are other rare instances of such agonizing prayer. Having received the "Spirit of his Son" we should not be surprised to find some who have experienced vigils of agonizing prayer,

fastings, wrestlings and labors in prayer. Great victories are born of such praying. This is the travail that brings forth true revival. Such prayer must certainly be "in the Holy Ghost." No professional charlatan would be willing to pay such a price. It is, as Paul expressed it, "According to his working, which worketh in me mightily."

There is no stated inflexible theorem that may be used like a charm to enable one to pray in the Holy Ghost. A few practical hints are offered:

1. Be sober. "Be ye therefore sober, and watch unto prayer" (1 Peter 4:7). It is not expected that those interested in effective prayer are at the same time given to inebriety, but there are other things beside alcohol which intoxicate and leave the mind too confused, exhausted and dulled for mutual communion with God.

It is not expected that the drunken debauchee may suddenly shift from his debauchery to a state of virtue and fellowship with God without the miracle that makes him a new creature. No one would expect him, without the great change, to participate in intercessory prayer. But there are things far less evil than strong drink which disqualify the Christian for communion with God. For example: business, excess in harmless pleasure, frivolity, pride, anger. Some of these are quite legitimate, but if excessively indulged in, they become harmful. Everyone knows how anger can disarm one and make him feel unfit to enter the place of prayer or the presence of God. Think how one must feel when business has robbed him of the privilege of keeping trust with God for prolonged periods of time, and someone suddenly calls urging him to pray the prayer of faith for a dying soul. Sobriety, temperance and moderation are in order for those who will do business with God successfully in prayer.

2. *"Wait upon the Lord"* (Isaiah 40:31). Do not be in a hurry. Do not rush into the place of prayer and rush out. It shows disrespect for Him. Someone has said that prayer is not "a hurried visit to a religious drive in, where one can grab a moral sandwich or a cup of spiritual stimulant" and be quickly on his way (Albert E. Day in *Existence Under God*). Most of us lament that we have so much to do that we cannot afford the time to pray, in which case we are admitting that we are willing to forfeit God's best for something temporal—something on the bargain counter—that will quickly pass away. Here is a place where one can do more by doing less. "Take time to be holy" and stand amazed at the wonderful way the Lord will take care of other things. "Seek ye first the kingdom of God and his righteousness and all these things shall be added unto you."

There should be seasons of "leisure" that we may give ourselves to prayer (1 Corinthians 7:5). It is while waiting upon the Lord and denying oneself the numerous carnal claims which bid for our time that one exposes himself to the Holy Spirit, thus giving him opportunity to help his infirmities and make supplications through him.

3. *Make prayer the business of life.* Said the Apostles, "We will give ourselves continually to prayer, and to the ministry of the word" (Acts 6:4). This was their answer to a crisis. Be like the devoted soldier that "waited on him (Cornelius) continually" (Acts 10:7). That was his assignment. Have you noticed with what strain some people pray when called upon unexpectedly, and with what ease and spontaneity others pray under similar circumstances? Some are unaccustomed to praying, while others make it a lifetime business. They are not strangers at the throne of grace.

"A ministry that is college-trained, but not Spirit-filled works no miracles. The church that multiplies committees and neglects prayer may be fussy, noisy, enterprising, but it labors in vain, and spends its strength for nought. It is possible to excel in mechanics and fail in dynamics. There is a superabundance of machinery; what is wanting is power . . . The real work of the church depends upon the power of the Spirit . . . When the church is run on the same lines as a circus, there may be crowds, but no Shekinah. That is why prayer is the test of faith and the secret of power. The Spirit of God travails in the prayer life of the soul. Miracles are the direct work of His power, and without miracles the church cannot survive. Education can civilize, but it is being born again that saves. The energy of the flesh can run bazaars, organize amusements and raise millions; but it is the presence of the Holy Spirit that makes a Temple of the Living God. The root trouble of the present distress is that the church has more faith in the world and the flesh than in the Holy Ghost . . . The breath of the four winds would turn death into life and dry bones into mighty armies, but it comes only by prayer."—Samuel Chadwick.

CHAPTER XI

THE PENTECOSTAL TEMPLE

TEMPLES of the Living God is the title of honor bestowed upon our lowly human person in the Word of God (1 Corinthians 3:16).

Since the fall of man and the accompanying cataclysmic results "the creature (the physical person) was made subject to vanity." It is far inferior to the perfect personalities of our first parents and also to our anticipated lot at the appearing of our Lord when we shall see Him face to face, for then "we shall be like him" (1 John 3:2). Presently we are hampered in our noblest pursuits because of the frailty of the "body of humiliation," "the body that belongs to our low estate, as Moffatt translates it (Philippians 3:21, Margin). Because of its transitory nature which is subject to the ravages of disease, time and death, Paul referred to the physical body as a "tabernacle" or "tent."

Notwithstanding his present lowly estate, man is still a noble creature, "fearfully and wonderfully made." Though he has fallen from the pristine, holy estate in which he bore the "image" of the Creator into a rebellious state of sin whose thoughts and imaginations are continually evil, God has not despised him. Sin has plundered and wasted him so that he is now only a faint resemblance of the man God created in the beginning. His mind has deteriorated from its original brilliance. His spirit has become dulled and has lost the fine sensibilities it had in the Edenic fellowship with God. But there is still something grand, even majestic, about him, something that God loves, something he has determined to salvage at the most extravagant cost. In his scheme of redemption he has spared no expense. "For God so loved the world, that he gave his only begotten Son, that whosoever believeth in him should not perish, but have everlasting life." He will have man restored and in redemption, through Jesus Christ, He offers him a grander place with Him than Adam ever knew.

Whatever may be said of man as he now is, God wants him as a temple of the Holy Ghost. There are limitless possibilities for him. God is not interested in temples made of marble and granite, or gold and silver bedecked with glittering jewels. He will have His law and His truth demonstrated in human temples which are his own "workmanship, created in righteousness and true holiness." The human temple is a great one, with many rooms, all of which when dedicated to God, reveal His excellence as it could never be revealed in temples made with hands.

I. In this imposing edifice there is the room of intellect. It is the thinking department where the mental processes are ceaselessly at work. It has "sought out many inventions." Here is the seat of reason and imagination. This department has unlimited potentialities for good or for evil, depending upon the character of the occupant of the temple. When it is out of control, the reason is distorted and the imaginations are evil continually. This is the room where all the plans of life are prepared to be presented to the executive department for final decision.

It is not strange that so many lives are frustrated, disorganized and disorderly when it is understood that so far as God and righteousness are concerned, the "spirit" of man is dead, past feeling, void of spiritual understanding (Ephesians 2:1; 4:18; 1 Corinthians 2:14).

The intellect eagerly awaits the coming of the divine occupant to set it in order, to save it from endless frustrations, and to preside over it, for the intellect of man is at its best when under the control of the Holy Spirit.

II. There is the room of memory, the department of archives of the temple, where all the records are kept—where an unerring hand keeps a true life record of all that happens from the cradle to the grave. It is often a "plunder room," but in it there is all the past in memory—everything we have seen, heard, read, experienced or thought, whether they be good or bad. Some things are so completely removed from our recollection that so far as we know they are dead. But there is no dead past. Every item is safely stored in the subconscious mind and very much alive, ready to spring into consciousness in an instant. When we visit friends of long ago and talk about other friends and times long gone from us, these moments suddenly seem to be alive again. Drowning persons, they tell us, see a whole panorama of their lives in a flash of time. Every detail is plainly preserved, just waiting to be called upon. The Holy Spirit has a way of causing us to remember at the proper time.

Memories of a wasted life will haunt one for eternity. To the rich fool in hell Abraham said, "Son, remember." Such memories will be like old wounds oozing with corruptions that made life unhappy and heaven impossible.

It was never the wish of the Supreme Architect that this should be the archives of evil, but that it should be a storehouse of precious memories, which are only possible when He who designed the temple for His own habitation is allowed to occupy it. The delectables of victorious living begin when He moves in. Memories of such a life are sweet.

III. The executive chamber of the magnificent temple is the will of man. Herein profound decisions are made—decisions which determine life and destiny. Tragically though, the will of natural man is forever at variance with the will of God. "The carnal mind is not subject to the law of God." Unless the will of man is mastered by the Master Himself the life cannot be a suitable temple for the Holy Ghost. In considering the claims of Christ Jesus upon our lives, it is not uncommon that the intellect agrees and admits that it is right and proper to submit and yield to Him. With this fact also the emotions agree, often with intense feeling and tears. Despite that, however, an obstinate will frequently vetoes, overrules, and rejects Christ. But when the will capitulates before him, the Lord will suddenly come to his temple. The will is the last part of man to surrender to Christ.

IV. Another room of interest to everyone is that of emotion. This is the arena of joys and sorrows, laughter and tears. It is the seat of love and hate. We may call it the sentimental department. A very important and popular room it is, for "the heart hath reasons that the reason does not know" (Pascal). This room is comparable to the grand ballroom, for it is the place of music where hearts sing and dance in the lilt of springtime. But it may quickly turn to be a place of grief and bitter weeping or hellish strife and war. Life on the human level is a potpourri of sweet and bitter, of delights and disappointments. But remember that He who "binds up the brokenhearted" and causes "the righteous to sing and rejoice" has a claim on this entire temple. His presence there will temper both our joys and sorrows.

V. The last room of the great temple which we shall mention is that of conscience. It is the legal department. Here the actions, thoughts, motives and decisions are weighed and investigated, and approved or disapproved. The conscience tries to find means to justify all we do, and if that is not possible he quickly and mercilessly condemns. He commends us when we do well, but when we have transgressed he lays on the lash of unmitigated justice, and allows no music in the grand ballroom. He speaks at length to the offender of the righteousness of God and his just demands upon our lives. Thereby keeping the guilty awake at night with his persistent preachments of "you ought" and "you ought not."

Be it said that insofar as he is enlightened, the conscience is always on God's side where moral issues are involved. He is a faithful monitor. He is not, however, an infallible guide, because there are areas in which he is not enlightened, and others in which he has been stifled so long his voice can not be heard. Give me a conscience void of offense. Such a conscience will acquiesce with the Word of God and submit to the guidance of the Holy Spirit. It will welcome the coming of the Spirit to preside over the temple, and will be most happy under his administration.

The Temple in Ruins

Though this magnificent human temple was designed as the dwelling place of the Most High, sin has prostituted it into the habitation of the enemies of God. The intellect yields to satanic influences and to his own "vile imagination." Its tremendous abilities dissipate themselves in selfish schemes, devilish mischief, devious and hateful vice, bloodshed and war. Memory is a charnel house of evil deeds, cursings, hatred and filthy stories. Robert Burns wrote: "My life reminds me of a ruined temple. What strength, what proportion in some parts. What unsightly gaps, what prostrate ruins in others" (*Promised Holy Spirit*, by William Barclay). In describing the life of the intellectual giant and patriot of American History, Daniel Webster, after he became the victim of his own vices, someone remarked: "What a magnificent ruin." No more pitiful sight is to be found than the stately, splendid temple of the Holy Ghost defiled and under the control of the arch-enemy of God and man. How fitting the words of Paul: "If any man defile the temple of God, him shall God destroy; for the temple of God is holy, which temple ye are" (1 Corinthians 3:17). The answer to the insatiable yearnings and pinings and hungerings for something—Who knows what?—is that the Divine Guest has not been invited to come in and live in the Temple which is His by right of creation and redemption.

Reason for the Human Temple

In order to enable us to appreciate the effectiveness of God's choice to supercede temples of stone with human temples, let us consider the ancient temple of Israel and try to determine God's purpose in having a temple in the first place.

The Temple of God in Jerusalem in the mind of the devout Israelite stood for all he knew, understood or believed about God. The literal presence of God was in the Temple. It was glorious because of all it represented in the history of the chosen people.

The Temple of Solomon was the pride of every citizen of Israel and there was much about it to make him justly proud. It was constructed at a cost that would be simply baffling in our day of inflated finance. One is astounded to know that there is not a building in America that cost as much as that Temple. The value of the precious metals alone has been calculated at $5,351,274,640. This takes no account of the brass and iron or the cost of labor used in its construction. This astronomical sum was reached by calculating the value of the gold at the rate of $20.67 per ounce. If this price seems a little high, one should figure it at the present rate of Gold, which is $36.00 per troy ounce. These figures were ascertained from A. J. Holman Dictionary and Concordance. The building was built of stones made ready at the quarry. Every stone and piece of timber was precision cut, marked and ready to be set in order when laid down at the building site in Jerusalem.

However, the cost and splendor of the temple is irrelevant except that it was typical of God's most precious possession, the church, which cost him incomparably more. The value he places on the church is infinitely greater, because it cost him his only begotten Son. He has ever expanding plans for the church in time and in eternity. It delights his heart to make known "the riches of the glory of his inheritance in the saints, And what is the exceeding greatness of his power to usward who believe, according to the working of his mighty power" (Ephesians 1:18, 19).

I. The Temple was the dwelling place of God. When the building was completed King Solomon and the congregation gathered in the court to dedicate it to the Lord. It must wholly belong to him. "And it came to pass, when the priests were come out of the holy place, that the cloud filled the house of the Lord, So that the priests could not stand to minister because of the cloud: for the glory of the Lord had filled the house of the Lord. Then spake Solomon, The Lord said that he would dwell in the thick darkness" (1 Kings 8:10-12). Thus did the glory—the Shekinah—appear. It was God's acknowledgment of the Temple dedicated to him. Thus did he honor it by the supernatural manifestation of his presence, as the place of which he had said, "My name shall be there" (1 Kings 8:29).

In like manner the physical temple must be dedicated to him. It is precious to him since it was redeemed by the precious blood of Christ. He must be acknowledged as Redeemer and Lord if we would have him acknowledge us.

II. The Temple was the specific place of God's manifestation. The manifestation of the glory was not a mere passing incident. The divine presence "between the cherubim" above the mercy seat remained constantly. Desiring to draw nigh to God the people came to the temple to worship and to make sacrifices. There they came to learn the Law and to receive God's blessing. It was the established place of worship. "In my distress I called upon the Lord, and cried to my God: and he did hear my voice out of his temple," said David (2 Samuel 22:7). The Law required the people to go to Jerusalem to worship, because the Temple was there. "Take heed to thyself that thou offer not thy burnt offerings in every place that thou seest: But in the place which the Lord shall choose" (Deuteronomy 12:13, 14). The Israelites were to bring the tithe to the Temple (Deuteronomy 14:23).

When in far away places the devout made their prayers facing the direction of the Temple. For the various festivals Jews from all over the known world, wherever they had been scattered, made long pilgrimages to Jerusalem, the Holy City, to worship in the Temple. Wherever events had taken them they remembered God as dwelling only in the Temple.

The dispersion of the Jews during the Babylonian captivity demonstrated how deeply entrenched the Temple worship was in their religious pattern, notwithstanding some very plain Scripture declaring the omnipresence of God. For instance, "Whither shall I go from thy spirit? or whither shall I flee from thy presence? If I ascend up into heaven, thou art there: if I make my bed in hell, behold, thou art there" (Psalm 139:7, 8). It also demonstrated their dire need of the new and more perfect revelation that the Messiah would bring. To them God dwelt in the Temple. Jerusalem was therefore the place where men ought to worship. Away from Jerusalem they felt they were away from God. In the light of this distorted idea of the omnipresent God it is easy to understand their sad plight as captives in Babylon when called upon to sing a song of Zion: "By the rivers of Babylon, there we sat down, yea, we wept, when we remembered Zion. We hanged our harps upon the willows in the midst thereof. For there they that carried us away captive required of us a song; and they that wasted us required of us mirth, saying, Sing us one of the songs of Zion. How shall we sing the Lord's song in a strange land? If I forget thee, O Jerusalem, let my right hand forget her cunning" (Psalm 137:1-5).

Manifestly, therefore, Israel was in urgent need of new light and of a more worthy concept of God. It was not that God had confused them, or had bound Himself to the Temple in Jerusalem, or that He was victim of a superstitious monopoly. Their concept of Him was too small. But "in due time" Christ came. His mission, along with seeking and saving the lost, was to "show us the Father," and to enable us to come to him. It was at this very point that he made a most revolutionary revelation of God. Addressing the unnamed woman at Jacob's well in Sychar he declared, "Woman, believe me, the hour cometh, when ye shall neither in this mountain, nor yet at Jerusalem, worship the Father . . . But the hour cometh, and now is, when the true worshippers shall worship the Father in spirit and in truth: for the Father seeketh such to worship him. God is a Spirit: and they that worship him must worship him in spirit and in truth" (John 4:21-24). If God is a Spirit he cannot be confined to any particular tribe, nation, shrine, ritual or denomination. If He is a universal Spirit, He is everywhere. This was a most progressive revelation of God, and was calculated to release them from their stinted idea of a tribal, national God, prisoner in his temple.

The New Testament Temple

"Know ye not that ye are the temple of God, and

that the Spirit of God dwelleth in you? If any man defile the temple of God, him shall God destroy; for the temple of God is holy, which temple ye are" (1 Corinthians 3:16, 17).

Since God is no longer interested in temples of insensible, unconscious marble and granite made with hands though they be creations of genius and grandeur, it is because the time has come that men and women—have become the media through which He chooses to manifest himself to the world. This represents a radical departure from the old regime of a presumptuous, spiritually blind priesthood which monopolized the Temple worship and prostituted it to a "den of thieves." At this point we should note that at Pentecost the Holy Spirit was not given in the Temple, but in an upper room of a residence. Since then it has no longer been necessary for mortal man to approach his maker via a human mediator or to make a pilgrimage to a particular shrine to meet him. The Holy Spirit was not poured upon a mediatorial system or upon the temple, but He came into lives of redeemed human beings. Now all may be filled with the Holy Spirit,[1] and everyone may become a

---

1. The phrases "baptized with the Holy Ghost" and "in the Holy Ghost" have been used interchangeably throughout this writing. "Baptized with the Holy Ghost" appears in Matt. 3:11, Mark 1:8, Luke 3:16, John 1:33, as the translation of the Greek *en pneumati hagio*. According to authorities either "in" or "with" is acceptable. In view of the literal meaning of the Greek word *baptizein* for baptize it is evident that the work of Christ, according to John, was to baptize "in the Holy Ghost." Those who receive the Pentecostal experience are virtually dipped in the Holy Ghost.

Also the phrase, "filled with the Holy Ghost" has been used synonymously

temple of God. Some might be deprived of going to the Temple, but none need forfeit the right to be a Temple of God. Stuart Holden has said, "Under the old dispensation God had a temple for his people, but under the new dispensation, he has his people for a temple."

Filled with the Spirit, the temple is under His control. The civil war is ended. The various departments of the temple are coordinate and enjoy a harmonious adjustment. The executive department—baptized, dipped, saturated, dyed in the Holy Ghost—acts in harmony with the will of God and thinks God's thoughts.

In such a temple God can display His glory. The living temple is the sphere of his manifestation. Here God manifests His truth, purity, tenderness, forgiveness, justice, love, mercy and holiness. Each member of the body is a holy vessel unto the Lord. By it his works are done, because the mortal body is quickened by the Spirit.

Such temples are the "Light of the world." Jesus referred to His body as a "temple." Of him it is writ-

---

with "baptized with the Holy Ghost." In defense of this terminology it will be seen that before Pentecost it was prophesied that "He shall baptize you with the Holy Ghost," while on the Day of Pentecost when it actually occurred the record merely states "They were all filled with the Holy Ghost," with no mention of the word *baptize*.

Prior to Pentecost there had been no "baptism in the Holy Ghost," yet many were said to have been "filled with the Holy Ghost." Since that time it appears that initially the candidate may be baptized with the Holy Ghost at which time he is also filled, and that subsequently he may be filled many times. (Note Acts 4:31). Those filled were the same baptized and/or filled in Acts 2:4.

ten, "In him was life; and the life was the light of men" (John 1:4). From human temple windows there streams the light of the world when the Spirit dwells within. The gleam of light that once beamed from his solitary earthly person is now multiplied by the millions of Spirit-filled persons. Thus it is ordained of God that all the world may see and glorify God.

God's people, therefore, are not only highly honored as being temples of God, but as a result of the gracious calling they are highly obligated. The gospel can only be preached through human lips. His work is best done by human hands. The love of God is made known only as it radiates from human hearts. The gospel light may be seen only as it is diffused through the Christian life. Unto us—not unto angels with trumpet voices—is committed the charge to preach the everlasting gospel.

The Lord, the Holy Ghost, is eager to occupy your temple. If he has not come in Pentecostal fullness, He awaits your complete consecration. Faith, love, obedience and full surrender are the requisites.

An internationally famous evangelical minister relates a most interesting experience in seeking and receiving the baptism in the Holy Ghost. He states that he had sought for the blessing ardently, but unsuccessfully for a long time. Returning home from a meeting where he had again been disappointed he knelt by a chair to seek further. He was physically exhausted with sheer fatigue and soon was fast asleep on his knees. There the Lord came and spoke to him in a dream. The conversation, though not verbatim, was as follows:

"So you want to be filled with the Holy Ghost?" questioned the Lord.

"Yes, more than anything in the world," was the honest reply.

"Then," said Jesus, "give me the keys to your house."

In the dream the earnest seeker said, "I saw myself forthwith hand over my ring of keys to him. Then with his eyes like a flame of fire penetrating me through and through, the Lord simply asked, "Are these all the keys?" It was a soul searching question.

Stunned by the directness of the question as well as by the look on his face, the seeker confessed, "Yes, all but one—the key to a very small room which I have reserved for private reasons." What was in the room he did not reveal. "Then," continued the seeker, "I saw the injured look on his countenance as he with obvious disappointment handed the keys back to me."

The dream ended, but its message was clear and poignant. Immediately the seeker awoke and lost no time in making the consecration complete and in delivering the other key. Then instantly the Holy Spirit came to fill the temple.

Those who would have Him occupy and dominate their lives must give Him all the keys and the control of their entire life. Failure to do so explains why so many Christians have not been filled with the Holy Ghost.

CHAPTER XII

PENTECOSTAL EXPERIENCE: ADAPTABLE AND INCLUSIVE

WHEN Israel at last moved into Canaan, the land was divided among them by lots, but it was incumbent on them to dispossess the Canaanites in order to possess their sections. This, to their sorrow, was never completely achieved. In like manner the baptism in the Holy Ghost is the possession of all of God's children though many of them never make much of an effort to claim their rights and to take their possession. Like the Israelites who were willing to compromise for a few acres when they could have had a whole section if they would have fought for it, numerous Christians are content to stop short of their inheritance, concluding spiritlessly, "I'm glad that Jesus saves me, And that's enough for me." Such hapless souls have surely underestimated their inheritance. Therefore, a re-evaluation of Pentecost and its blessings for today as being adaptable to our needs and including "as many as the Lord our God shall call," is in order.

It is significant that before Jesus concluded His
ministry and just before His suffering and death, He
unfolded the doctrine of the personal coming of the
Comforter to dwell personally in the hearts of His
disciples, and that directly after He was risen from
the dead, He resumed the subject at the first
meeting with the disciples. After a word of cheerful
greeting He said, "Receive ye the Holy Ghost" (John
20:22). This was on the very day of His resurrection while the disciples were still hiding behind barred
doors for fear of the Jews. During the forty days He
was with them the subject of the coming of the Holy
Ghost as it concerned the kingdom of God was the
distinctive message. His last words to them immediately preceding the ascension was: "And, behold, I
send the promise of my Father upon you: but tarry
ye in the city of Jerusalem, until ye be endued with
power from on high" (Luke 24:49). The same message with some amplification is recorded in Acts
1:4-8, which also states: "But ye shall receive power,
after that the Holy Ghost is come upon you: and ye
shall be witnesses unto me both in Jerusalem, and in
all Judaea, and in Samaria, and unto the uttermost
part of the earth." That was the final blessing of
Jesus, and as He finished speaking "a cloud received
him out of their sight."

The strategic times at which He spoke of the coming of the Comforter, just before His death, immediately after His resurrection, and just as He was

about to ascend to the Father—certainly add force to the significance of the entire subject. Last moments and farewells are not times for meaningless verbosity, and if Jesus had ever indulged in it, it would not have been on such a momentous occasion. Last words of friends usually make a lasting impression on the listener, and certainly the last words of Jesus spoken on earth should have made an indelible impression on the hearers. This subject should therefore receive from all Christians the same reverence and consideration the disciples gave it. To fail here, at least in a measure, is to dishonor Him.

I. Jesus realized that the success of His cause depended upon men rightly trained and qualified. He had chosen the disciples and had been for a period of three and a half years their Divinity Tutor. Their training had been superb and unequaled. The statement in Acts 4 that they "were ignorant and unlearned" refers only to formal education or rabbinical training. But no matter how well they had been trained, even at the feet of the Master, that was not enough. Though having been chosen by Christ and having been graduated from His school, they must receive the Holy Ghost. Other qualifications, gifts or abilities would not suffice.

Love, some say, is the desideratum. The disciples loved Jesus and had forsaken all to follow him, but their enthusiastic love for him though executed in pure, unselfish service could never take the place of the Comforter. It was clear to them that they must receive the Holy Ghost. Lacking the Pentecostal experience, they would not qualify for the extraordinary responsibility of promoting the Master's cause.

II. Many are of the opinion that the success of the Church is dependent upon the authority of its ministry. No expense is spared to see to it that the ministers are properly ordained, and that often with pompous ceremony. Never were men commissioned with greater authority—authority from the Lord Himself—than that given to the Twelve. He had individually chosen them, trained them, commissioned them. Theirs was the ordination of the nail-pierced hands, by the Bishop of our Souls, the Head of the Church.

But these men, so signally honored, understood that everything depended upon their obedience to His command to "Tarry . . . until ye be endued with power from on high." Their high sounding titles—apostles, bishops, elders—were nil unless they received that power. Without an exception they were convinced that they should receive the Holy Ghost before proceeding to evangelize the world.

The promise of the Father to pour out the Spirit upon all flesh without a doubt was intended for every child in the family of God, because everyone was expected to be a witness for Christ. Everyone is therefore eligible. God will countenance no display of carnal ability. Witnessing for Him was never intended to be an exhibition of human personality, pulpit psychology, or plying of the preaching art. The "excellency of the power" must be of God. His message was to be proclaimed with the "Holy Ghost sent down from heaven" (see 1 Corinthians 2). As long as, and wherever the gospel is preached, the command of the Saviour, "Receive ye the Holy Ghost," is in order.

III. Since it is the purpose of God as well as His gracious provision that everyone should receive the baptism in the Holy Ghost, it follows that the Holy Ghost is adaptable to every type of human personality. The personality will in every instance be improved when the Holy Ghost has come to guide it into paths of truth. The weak and timid person under His influence becomes bold, strong and courageous. Special talents or native genius, or lack of them, is no excuse for failure to receive the Holy Ghost, because whatever the natural graces may be, the entire personality will be enhanced when consecrated to God and yielded to the guidance and control of the Holy Ghost. In support of this position let us examine a cross section of personalities of the first followers of Jesus before and after Pentecost.

1. Peter's life is a good example of the transformation Pentecost brings. Impulsiveness is his out-

standing characteristic. He is a representative of that type of person who makes quick decisions and proceeds with driving force. Knowing their own minds, and on the impulse of an instant without taking time to consider the consequences, they spring into action. Right or wrong, they are quick to act or to speak.

Peter was a man of action—often wrong—but one of action nevertheless. When Jesus walking on the stormy sea appeared to the disciples, while the others were thinking it over, Peter immediately cried, "Lord, if it be thou, bid me come unto thee on the water." As soon as Jesus had bidden him to come, Peter was over the side of the boat, and was very soon overwhelmed by the waves. But at least he acted, though impulsively.

On the Mount of Transfiguration it was he who spoke up without knowing what he said, "Let us build three tabernacles." He had spoken when silence would have been golden.

Without understanding what was really involved he pledged his all to Jesus, vowing that though all others forsake Him, he would die with Him rather than forsake Him, a vow we know now he was unable to keep. In his conceit he rebuked the Lord so that Jesus countered sharply, "Get thee behind me Satan."

His impulsiveness must have resulted in much embarrassment to himself and to others. It required much explaining at times. But that was his pattern of behavior—act and explain later. Sometimes it brought him deep sorrow and bitter tears.

But Peter was not ruled out by his impulsiveness. Jesus made it clear to him that he was counting on him to be a witness unto him, though he had denied the Lord with cursings, and had shamefully forsaken him. To what a low state he had fallen! A witness, indeed! How unfit he felt for such service. How could he ever become a living witness of Jesus? He knew he needed something that would give him poise, something that would take the place of his variable vacillations, something that would harness his impulsiveness for the glory of God. He needed to be healed of his imbalance.

Jesus had the answer. His command which was addressed to everyone was personally directed to Peter. His case was not impossible, nor was he exempt because of any native ability. He was to receive the Holy Ghost. The Pentecostal blessing included him and was adaptable to his particular need.

The pre-Pentecostal picture is of *Petros* the small stone. Henceforth, according to the prophecy of Jesus, he should be called *Petra*, a large mass of rock. The post-Pentecostal picture reveals him as a steadfast granite rock—Peter filled with the Holy Ghost.

2. There has been considerable misapprehension about the Apostle John. Because of the gentle, benign side of his character which is chiefly post- Pen-

tecostal, he has sometimes been overrated. Because he describes himself as "that disciple whom Jesus loved" and because he leaned on the breast of Jesus at the Last Supper, we have taken much for granted about him. Also in the caption of the Book of Revelation some translator has ascribed to him the title of "St. John the Divine." That is certainly a misnomer. He was emphatically not divine, and did not profess to be.

John has often been described as an impetuous person. If we agree that Peter was impulsive, we do no violence to John to agree that he was impetuous. That means he was the type person who often expresses himself with rushing force and violence, often with fury. John seems to have been a very independent, self-reliant, capable man. He was both ardent and vehement. It was not without some valid reason that he and his brother James were nicknamed Sons of Thunder. He was very zealous for the Lord and his convictions were firm and deep rooted. While there was tenderness about his personality, he could also flame with indignation. It was he who proposed calling fire down from heaven to consume a village in Samaria for rejecting the message of Jesus.

No one would have more readily acknowledged his need of the promised Comforter than John. He knew he needed what Jesus had prescribed, and he was not exempt from the command, receive the Holy Ghost. Only in that Spirit and power would he dare venture forth on the career of preaching the gospel. The Pentecostal blessing suited his personality exactly.

Many today are like John. They possess wonderful virtues and are very zealous for the Lord. Their standards are so well defined and clear that they can scarcely tolerate any defection in others. They are ready to call the vengeance of God upon all offenders. But they, like John, need to hear the tender solicitation of Jesus, "Receive ye the Holy Ghost." He will impart a heavenly quality of character that will temper our high metal and dispose us to moderation.

3. The New Testament affords us little information concerning the character of James. However, from what we do have, we gather that he appears to have been a strong man of commanding, authoritative, officious, legalistic stature. "Imperative" seems to be the word which describes him. He walked punctiliously and wanted others to do the same. There seems to be an air of austerity about him. Whether this description of him is accurate or not, Jesus advised him also to receive the Holy Ghost. That is the up-to-date answer to legalists of all time. The coming of the Holy Ghost will disarm the driver of the whip and remove the compulsion of Law, in order that he may know the constraining power of love shed abroad in the heart by the Holy Ghost.

4. Thomas, the incredulous, is well known to all

of us. Much could be said in his favor in spite of his honest doubts. He seems to have possessed a deep sense of loyalty for the Lord until the great trial came, when he along with the others forsook him and fled. He appears to have been a strong man with a somber disposition, always fearing the worst.

The personality of Thomas has been depicted in a famous work of art by Thorwaldson, in which he is represented as a grave, thoughtful person, standing in a skeptical attitude, holding a rule in his hand, ready to measure everything for himself. In this respect he is representative of all honest doubters.

For some unknown reason he was absent at the meeting when Jesus first appeared to the ten disciples after the Resurrection. Maybe he brooded over the loss of Jesus and over the role he and his colleagues had so ignobly played during the awful trial. In his melancholy he may have preferred to be alone. But he missed the unspeakable privilege of seeing the risen King. And when he heard the good news from those who did see him, he could not believe it. He had seen the Saviour taken from the cross and sealed in the tomb, and it certainly was unscientific to believe that in so short a time He was alive again. The story was incredulous. Perhaps the others were victims of hallucinations. John had believed when he had entered the empty tomb and had seen the grave clothes lying undisturbed and in order. But Thomas honestly could not believe the story of the other ten or of

Mary Magdalene or of Cleopas and his companion. He contended that he must see and feel for himself. He was just another honest skeptic.

The Lord is interested in honest doubters. On the following Sunday when all were together, including Thomas, Jesus appeared again. Confronted with the living person of Jesus, his doubts all fled, and he exclaimed in humble contrition, "My Lord and my God!" To be cured of doubt concerning the Resurrection of Jesus is a gracious experience, but that is not enough. Thomas too, must "Tarry . . . until endued with power from on high." This is a fitting experience for all practical men.

5. In our cross sectional view of the followers of the Lord who were commanded to receive the Holy Ghost, the last will be the impeccable virgin mother Mary. Such a person is one not liable to sin knowingly. She, of all women that ever lived, was the one chosen of God to become the mother of His Son. The angel Gabriel when sent from God to visit Mary greeted her with the beautiful words, "Hail, thou that art highly favored, the Lord is with thee: blessed art thou among women." Nevertheless, this holy woman, so favored of the Lord, was required to receive the Holy Ghost.

From the last earthly meeting of Jesus with His followers on the Mount of Olives from whence they saw Him ascending through the clouds Mary was among those who remembered and obeyed the command that they should not depart from Jerusalem, but should wait for the promise of the Father. The inspired record reads, "These all continued with one accord in prayer and supplication, with the women, and Mary the mother of Jesus, and with his brethren" (Acts 1:14). This is the last mention of Mary in the New Testament, but it affords us an inspiring picture of her and her sons, James, Joses, Simon and Judas—all together en route to the appointed meeting to wait for the coming of the Comforter. It is a glowing picture of their faith in Mary's greater Son, their brother, who in the language of Mary was "God, my Saviour." The holy family dared not miss that eventful meeting. They were present when "The Day of Pentecost was fully come." Our last earthly view of her is in that meeting described in Acts 2, tarrying with the others, with upraised hands, a tongue of fire upon her head, being filled with the Holy Ghost.

Our brief cross sectional examination of personalities reveals one central truth—the baptism in the Holy Ghost is for all and is adaptable to every type of human personality. It is prescribed for the worthy and for the unworthy. No one can know God's best for him who disregards the command to receive the Holy Ghost.

Who then is so great, or mighty, or gifted, or so holy that he should by-pass Pentecost? Who can honestly say, "I do not need the Pentecostal gift?" What minister of the gospel would not be a more successful one if he obeyed the command, "Receive ye the Holy Ghost"? In view of all the successes anyone has known, how much greater might they have been if wrought in the energy of the Holy Ghost?

CHAPTER XIII

PERENNIAL PENTECOST

Our purpose in writing at length on Pentecost and the extraordinary manifestations of the Holy Spirit that launched the new church so triumphantly on its way has not been to afflict the reader with a despairing nostalgia for a past which is irretrievably gone or which is recoverable only by retrospection. If the realities and victories of the Holy Spirit are no longer available, all that has been said on the subject can serve no practical or worthy purpose. It is this writer's contention that the ministry of the Spirit in Pentecostal fullness according to the Pentecostal pattern is to continue until the end of the age, that is, until the Lord returns.

"Pentecost," says L. R. Scarborough, D.D., LL.D., in *Products of Pentecost,* "was not a religious pageant, nor a religious exhibition . . . It was God's inauguration of a world plan of evangelism, and was meant to carry through his kingdom until the King returns."

Said Jonathan Edwards, "Pentecost was not even the pattern day, but simply the start of Christianity."

If his judgment was correct Pentecost was indeed the norm of Christianity.

"We must regard Pentecost as, not an event, but the beginning of a process; not a transference of the Holy Ghost from heaven to earth, or a gift once for all bestowed upon the church, not a legacy of the dead to the living, but the opening of a river of life, the beginning of a flow of the Spirit in a current of communication from the Father to the Son, and from the incarnate Son to his body . . . So the descent of the Spirit is not an incident, but a constant process."—*What Happened at Pentecost*, Henry J. Wortherspoon, D.D.

Many excellent Bible scholars say the baptism in the Holy Spirit at Pentecost was the first and last needful outpouring of the Spirit upon the Church, but Scripture and experience agree that there is yet a personal need and that that need is met in the "enduement of power" so graciously promised to the Church in the beginning and guaranteed to continue until the end of the age.

Some scholars maintain, but without scriptural warrant, that the Pentecostal enduement of power expired with limitation. The promise which brought Pentecost, however, bore no date of limitation, and only awaits believing hearts for verification. Unbelief cannot make void any of the promises of God. It only impoverishes the unbeliever.

It was because Jesus was departing from the disciples bodily that he proposed sending another Comforter to take His place, though the promise had been made long before through the prophets. Because in the days of His flesh Jesus was restricted and hampered by a corporeal body, Jesus said, "It is expedient for you that I go away: for if I go not away, the Comforter will not come unto you; but if I depart, I will send him unto you" (John 16:7). As long as he is bodily absent the "enduement of power" in the universal person of the Holy Ghost will remain with the Church.

A few scriptural reasons proving that there has been no change in God's plan to "endue" the Church with the power of the Holy Ghost perennially are adduced here:

1. "The promise is unto you, and to your children, and to all that are afar off, even as many as the Lord our God shall call" (Acts 2:39). Could the promise be more inclusive? Does it outlaw any believer in Christ? Without a question this promise belongs essentially to the faith once for all delivered unto the saints, for which Jude so urgently exhorted us to "Earnestly contend" (Jude 3). It certainly belongs to our Christian heritage.

2. Jesus said, "But ye shall receive power, after that the Holy Ghost is come upon you: and ye shall be witnesses unto me . . . unto the uttermost part of the earth" (Acts 1:8). It is perfectly evident that

the promise was not limited to the then living disciples. They did not reach the "uttermost part of the earth" involved in the Master's program. As long as the church is in the world its mission will be the execution of and the extending of that program, and as long as the church has a mission of bearing witness the promise of the Holy Ghost enduement of power as an enablement will be valid and attainable. "And this gospel of the kingdom shall be preached in all the world for a witness unto all nations; and then shall the end come" (Matthew 24:14). Inasmuch as the end has not come the Church continues its mission of teaching, preaching, witnessing, and has every right to depend upon the promise of the Father for the Spiritual enduement of power. The promise runs concurrently with the Great Commission, which is in effect "unto the end of the age." There was no hint in the great commission that the plan would be altered for the modern age or that witnesses for Christ in the last days would require less of the divine authentication than their predecessors. The need is certainly as great as ever before. The commission was simply, "Go ye therefore, and teach all nations, baptizing them in the name of the Father, and of the Son, and of the Holy Ghost: Teaching them to observe all things whatsoever I have commanded you: and, lo, I am with you alway, even unto the end of the world. Amen" (Matthew 28:19, 20). How would He be present with them? He had promised, "I will not leave you comfortless: I will come to you" (John 14:18). And He did come to them in the marvelous miracle and manifestation of the Pentecostal power.

3. Jesus said that we should go to all nations "Teaching them to observe all things whatsoever I have commanded you." How could an ambassador of Christ be loyal to his commission if he omitted so pertinent a command as the one so clearly and so variously emphasized as the one: "Receive ye the Holy Ghost"? Certainly this was one of the things to teach believers to observe.

4. According to the prophecy of Joel (2:28-31) the outpouring of the Holy Ghost was to continue until the sun is turned to darkness and the moon to blood. That will be until the Lord returns.

5. The promise of the Father will continue to be in force as long as the Church is on earth. The promise is especially to the Church, because it is the "habitation of God through the Spirit" (Ephesians 2:22). The Church is dependent upon the power of the Spirit to carry out the Great Commission. The Church is far more than an assembly of people. Without the presence of the Holy Ghost, though it have all the doctrines and ordinances of the New Testament, it could never be the Church. The Church can never be satisfied with less than the Lord promised. As late as thirty years after the Day of Pentecost Paul was still

exhorting, "Be filled with the Spirit" (Ephesians 5:18). Certainly the Apostle was in harmony with the Master's program, and he knew of no expiration by limitation.

The Acts of the Apostles is a continuation of "All that Jesus began to do and to teach" as recorded in the Gospel according to Luke, the author of both books. The Gospel of Luke is his account of the life and acts of Jesus Christ while on earth. The Book of Acts is the record of the manner in which He carries on His work since His return to the Father and the sending of the Holy Ghost, the Comforter. The book might well have been titled "The Acts of the Holy Ghost." It is the "Acts of the Apostles" only in so far as they were indwelt and motivated by the Holy Ghost. It is the fascinating account of the fulfillment of the Lord's own words, "Greater works than these shall he do; because I go unto my Father" (John 14:12).

That the Comforter was the Enabler in advancing the work of the Lord Jesus Christ after His bodily ascension is quite obvious from the tenor of the entire Book of Acts. The numerous worthy feats of record were all accomplished through men indwelt and empowered by the Holy Ghost. It is noteworthy however that the Holy Spirit in no wise appropriates the honor to himself, always turning the spotlight upon Jesus. Notice a few pertinent examples: "They (apostles) went forth, and preached every where, the

Lord working with them" (Mark 16:20). "The Lord added to the church daily such as should be saved" (Acts 2:47). It was God's Son, Jesus, who healed the lame man at the Temple Gate (Acts 2:11). It was his Son, Jesus, whom God having raised from the dead sent to bless Israel, "in turning away every one of you from his iniquities" (Acts 3:26). To those who were being healed through the apostolic ministry the message was, "Jesus Christ maketh thee whole" (Acts 9:34). It is Christ who by the Spirit worketh among us. It was the prayer of Paul that the Ephesians and all Christians might know "the exceeding greatness of his power to usward who believe," all of which is resident in Christ Jesus, since it has pleased the Father to put all things under his feet, and who has exalted him above all, to be the Head of the Church (Ephesians 1), and that "in him should all fulness dwell" (Colossians 1:19).

The Holy Spirit is forever actively engaged in "confirming the Word," in empowering those who bear witness, in "convicting the world of sin, righteousness and judgment," but He is ever delighted to give all the glory to Jesus. Said Jesus, "He shall glorify me." He speaks not of himself, but of the crucified, risen Saviour. Jesus said, "He shall take of mine, and shall shew it unto you" (John 16:14, 15). Therefore, the Book of Acts is indeed the continued story of Jesus immediately after his ascension through the ministry of the Holy Ghost who came upon the waiting disciples according to the promise of Jesus.

However, this intriguing narrative of the glorious history of the Life of Christ through the Holy Ghost in the Church only covers a period of approximately thirty years. It certainly does not purport to be a complete account of all the acts of the Holy Ghost. Nor should anyone imagine that the acts of the Holy Ghost ceased with the ending of this Book.

The manner in which the Book ends is distinctly unique. In no sense is there a summation of the characters whose names appear therein. It closes abruptly on a rather low note, with one of the principals of the Church and of the Book a prisoner in Rome, rejected of his own countrymen, carrying on his ministry in a very cramped and limited way, in a rented house, anticipating execution though himself full of faith, exulting that "the Word of the Lord is not bound." In fact Acts ends so abruptly that one wonders whether the author had not intended to write further.

The only logical explanation of this fact is that Luke was an inspired writer, that he wrote only as he was "moved upon by the Holy Ghost" and ceased to write when the Spirit bade him stop. The written narrative ended, but the acts of the Holy Ghost continued. The sublime narration so suddenly terminated leaves one with the intense feeling that there should be a footnote, to be "continued." Surely such a story should be continued. History attests that the acts of the Holy Ghost have never ceased. The world is too small for an unabridged edition of all His mighty and endless deeds. Nevertheless the edition runs until this hour. This writer has only been concerned in clearly and fairly stating the Bible teaching on this subject, and shall not impose upon the readers the other proof of His present day wonders which are available in superabundance. But every Spirit-filled life is another chapter of the acts of the Holy Ghost. The Church of Pentecost perseveres to this day and continues to write voluminously of His wondrous acts—not on parchments or in paper books alone, but in visible lives of redeemed men and women. The world is challenged to read and to discover that Christ lives and that His power has not diminished.

"That grace of His which was shed so plentifully on the believers of the first days, is not an intermittent radiance, like the flash of a human eye, but is steady as the glory which streams from the face of the sun. Waning or exhaustion it does not know; and from age to age, from generation to generation, His saints will grow more and more mature, human life will increasingly reflect the glory of the Lord, and display His power to make weak mortals beset with temptation, meet to be partakers of the inheritance of the saints in light."—William Arthur, M.A., in *The Tongue of Fire*.

BIBLIOGRAPHY

Baptism With the Holy Ghost, R. A. Torrey.

Bible Doctrines, P. C. Nelson, Gospel Publishing House (Springfield, Mo.).

Christ of Every Road, E. Stanley Jones.

Evangelism, Old and New, A. C. Dixon.

Fullness of the Blessing, Evan H. Hopkins.

Fullness of Life, J. Stewart Holden, M.A., D.D.

He That Is Spiritual, Lewis Sperry Chaffer.

Holy Spirit, A. B. Simpson.

Ministry of the Spirit, A. J. Gordon.

Pentecostal Papers, or the Gift of the Holy Ghost, S. A. Keen, D.D.

Pillars of Pentecost, Charles W. Conn.

Spirit of Christ, Charles R. Erdman.

The Tongue of Fire, William Arthur, M.A.

The Way to Pentecost, Samuel Chadwick.

What Meaneth This, Carl Brumback.

What Happened at Pentecost, Henry J. Worthspoon, D.D.